CELTIC

ANTHOLOGY

A Collection of Short Stories, Poems & Memories

Written by

Celtic Fans

To

Mark,

Thankyou for all your
support over the years.
You've been the best
boss ever!
Lots of love T xx

Poems Crack, Fireworks, Yon Night @ Tom Leonard, from Outside the Narrative: Poems 1965-2009, Etruscan Books/ Word Power.

Another Planet @ Stephen O'Donnell, from Paradise Road, Ringwood Publishing.

Front and Back Cover copyright of Barry McGonigle

ISBN-13: 978-1493694389

ISBN-10: 1493694383

Contents

Celtic Anthology

Contents

Celtic Anthology

Contents

Celtic Anthology

Introduction

The art of storytelling has always been part of Celtic (Keltic) heritage. Stories were traditionally passed tongue to ear from one generation to the next through the local Seanachaidh (shawn-ah-key). Some Seanachaidh were travelling folk moving from community to community offering their skills in exchange for food and temporary shelter. Others were members of settled communities and told their tales at ceremonies and other local events. All were held in high esteem by the Irish and Scots who revered and cultivated story and song as their principal means of artistic and cultural expression.

Nothing was written. The history of the people was memorised in lyrical poems and songs recited by these bards. Each employed a range of storytelling conventions, styles of speech and gestures peculiar to the Celtic folk tradition and characterised them as practitioners of their art.

These ancient storytellers told their tales around dimly lit firesides, shadowy rock pools, or wherever an audience gathered to listen and learn. In Celtic mythology these oral masterpieces possessed special powers. Their words, filled with a sense of spirituality and power of otherworldly forces beyond the five senses, shaped beliefs buried deep within and satisfied a hunger for knowledge of the past. Fuelled by a sense of communion with the land and eternal presence of ancestors the Celtic people were, through the centuries, fed on a rich diet of legend and myth to feed the soul.

When a Marist monk called Brother Walfrid started a football club in the East End of Glasgow in 1888 there was only one name on his mind: Celtic; chosen to reflect the club's Irish roots and Scottish ambitions. Some wanted Emerald or Harp in the name, others fought for Glasgow Hibernian. Walfrid won the day but the fusion of Scottish and Irish cultures meant Celtic became known as Seltik rather than Keltic, as that was how local Glaswegians pronounced it.

Walfrid initially founded the club as a fundraising enterprise to help alleviate the poverty suffered by the working-class Irish immigrant community trying to settle in a new land. Forced to live in overcrowded, poor quality housing, and starved of food as well as employment, they

7

faced open hostility from large sections of the indigenous Scottish population.

Walfrid's dream was more than just a football club. It was about acceptance, hope and self-belief. He longed to create a vehicle which could provide not only dinners for the impoverished children but a recreation and release to raise the spirits of Glasgow's Irish community. It was the beginning of a story that would echo around the globe and inspire generations.

It's imperative for all fans to remember, and worth reiterating over and over to the many new fans attracted to the club, that when Celtic Football Club were born, they were born for a purpose, a people and a cause.

Celtic are now a global club with players and fans from around the world. They have tasted success on the field of play in Scotland and Europe, and shown the world how to play football the Celtic Way: a brand of free-flowing, attacking football with a natural philosophy - we'll score more goals than you. They entertain fans in a modern sixty thousand all-seater stadium that is the envy of many clubs. Top players are paid in a week what many fans do not earn in a year. This economic gulf has led to criticism of the club. Some have accused the club of being out of touch with its traditional core support: the poor, disenfranchised working-class inhabitants of Glasgow's East End, many of whom can't afford to put food on their family's dinner table never mind take them to watch games at Celtic Park.

But much of the work the club does for various charities goes unseen, including helping the latest influx of immigrants who have fled to Glasgow from various trouble spots around the world. For as Jock Stein once said, 'It's not the creed or nationality that counts.'

There is a reawakening of the club's original charitable ethos. The Celtic FC Foundation aims to improve the lives of the poorest and most vulnerable all over the world. Since its inception, it has raised in excess of £5million for a host of worthy causes. The Foundation also works in association with a wide range of organisations providing activities for people of all ages to engage in sport, health and education programmes in the wider community.

The Celtic Music Programme helps school kids learn about tolerance, inclusion, tradition and excellence through the medium of music. The Kibera Project is funding and providing labour for the building of a school in Kenya. Closer to home the Foundation is working closely with local partners to help put food on the dinner tables of the poor in Glasgow.

Motivated by the spirit of Walfrid the Celtic Anthology aims to breathe new life into the ancient art of Celtic storytelling for modern times and donate proceeds from the book sales to the Celtic FC Foundation. To help achieve these goals we've collected various tales and poems from around the world. Many stories are told in English. Others, in an attempt to capture a wide range of diverse voices, are written in various styles of the local dialect heard on the streets of Glasgow and the stands of Celtic Park. These voices, heard over the years singing and roaring Celtic teams to glory, have seldom been represented in the vast canon of literature relating to the club, yet they represent the roots of the Celtic support.

Reading the book will take you on a journey from the club's humble, but ambitious, beginnings to the challenges faced and conquered over the last one hundred and twenty five years. You will learn something different of legends that have played their part in creating the history you know today. You will laugh and cry at tales of humour and sadness. Most of all you will feel pride at being part of something special: the Celtic family. It doesn't matter if you're a season ticket holder or live on the other side of the world and have never stepped foot inside Celtic Park, if your heart is with Celtic you're part of the Celtic family.

It would be impossible for every one of our budding Seanachaidhs to orally share their stories around camp fires or schools. That's not to say such events won't be organised in the future.

Feel free to read these stories and poems aloud to a gathered audience anywhere on the globe, whether around a camp fire or to your children in bed at night. At the end of this journey together we hope you, your audience and your children become inspired to share your own stories and let your voice be heard. We are all a potential Seanachaidh. Everyone has a story to tell. How many times have you sat and listened to someone reciting a humorous or sad tale, whether at work, home or in the local pub? Perhaps you've told a similar tale yourself. Someone in the audience might have said that should be written down. More often than not you'll have used, or heard, the reply, 'Och, I don't know how to write.' For that reason many stories may be lost unless we do something about it. Don't let fear prevent you from recording your memories. Whether you do it for yourself, your children or grandchildren, or for a book or website, do what it takes. Add your voice and join the growing number of Seanachaidh.

If you enjoy the stories and poems in this book we hope you'll help spread the word and encourage others to get involved. Whether that entails buying further copies of the book as presents, or writing a story, or poem, or song, or whatever inspires you or future generations, is up to you.

Walfrid's Dream

Pat Marrinan

There's a quiet corner of Scotland far from the roaring crowd

Where a simple grave marks out a life not haughty, rich or proud

Here lies an Irish dreamer who heard his children cry

For want of food, or warmth or love and dared to question why?

He raged against the hunger, he railed against the hate

It tore his heart asunder when he saw their empty plates

But dreams can't feed these children so in his mind was born

A scheme to found a football club to take the world by storm

So a band of men he gathered and told them of his scheme

A community was put to work to build up Walfrid's dream

And the little ones had food again and the older ones had pride

From far and wide they came to see his marvellous Celtic side

They carved a place of honour and they met with destiny

From Celtic Park to Lisbon's sun it was plain for all to see

That Walfrid's dreams had all come true but yet he wanted more

As the wind-blown grass around his grave heard the distant roar

He would smile on all the glory his famous club had won

He'd be glad his people's children left the shadows for the sun

But he'd point to all those others who hunger here today

Will we watch their trials and struggles and mutely walk away?

11

There's a quiet corner of Scotland far from the roaring crowd

Where a simple grave marks out a life not haughty, rich or proud

The man has gone to his reward but his dream it echoes still

For children still need food today, will you help their plates to fill?

Those Few Days

Krys Kujawa

45,654. That's the number of days between Celtic's very first fixture on May 28th 1888 in a friendly against Rangers and Celtic's last game of their 125th anniversary season: the Scottish Cup final and the victory over Hibernian.

While that 5-2 victory back in 1888 may not have seemed like it at the time, it was the beginning of a truly amazing story. There was nothing up for grabs that day of course, just an opening fixture for a brand new team against a fellow Glasgow club and then off for a celebration between both teams afterwards to toast the beginning.

The 3-0 victory over Hibernian 45,653 days later was different of course, as Celtic lifted the Scottish Cup for a record 36th time. No club has lifted Scotland's oldest trophy more, and yet when you look at those numbers - 36 to 45,654 - it seems so small by comparison.

Throw in 44 League Championship winning days and 14 League Cup final victories and it takes our "big three" winning days up to 94. Then there's the other trophies Celtic have won over the years. 29 Glasgow Cups before it became a youth tournament. 26 Glasgow Charity Cups before it came to an end in 1961. That's us up to 149 winning days. 150 when you throw in our one and only Dryborough Cup victory in 1974.

There were two North Eastern cups in 1889 and 1890, one British League Cup in 1902, the Ferencvaros Vase in 1914, the Navy and Army War Fund Shield in 1918, the Empire Exhibition Cup in 1938, the Victory in Europe Cup in 1945, the Saint Mungo Cup in 1951, the Coronation Cup in 1953... the list of one-off cups goes on for a bit right up to the Wembley Cup in 2009 and the Fenway Football Challenge in 2010. But all of those don't even get us close to 200. Not even 0.5% of that 45,654.

Admittedly, not all of those days actually had a game involving Celtic. Indeed, most of them didn't. But that doesn't mean that those days didn't involve Celtic somewhere along the line. I'm fairly sure I'm not alone when I say that, even through the close season when there are no Celtic matches at all, there isn't a day goes by where I don't have some conversation with someone about something related to Celtic.

The fact of the matter is supporting a football club like Celtic isn't just about the games themselves, just as the games themselves aren't just about winning. Although in both cases that is ultimately the point. We don't care if we win, lose or draw... but given the choice we'd still rather they won! So when it comes to the days that we win the trophies, they should never be taken for granted.

That's not to say they don't all have their own merits which mean we remember some of those few days with more affection than others. The day Pierre Van Hooijdonk's goal beat Airdrieonians and ended a six year long wait for a trophy is massive for me because I don't really remember Celtic winning a major trophy before that. No doubt more important, though, was the day Henrik Larsson and Harald Brattbakk finally let us say "Cheerio to ten in a row!"

But I can only imagine what it was like being at the biggest win of all. The one I haven't mentioned to this point because it scarcely needs mentioning. Lisbon.

There might be less than 200 days of winning trophies in those 45,654, but May 25th 1967 is the shining beacon among all of those tens of thousands of days. I'm too young to have been around then, but we all know what that day meant. It's a day passed on through the generations, and a day we all cherish whether we were there or not.

I find it difficult to believe the achievement of the Lisbon Lions will ever be topped. Football just doesn't work like that anymore. Barcelona may have quite a few home-grown Catalans in their wonderful Champions League winning sides, but they've still got the Argentinian Lionel Messi and the Brazilian Dani Alves. The furthest afield you have to go to find a Lisbon Lion is Saltcoats, a mere 30 miles from Glasgow.

Yet the fact that achievement was so fantastic shouldn't take away from the achievements of other Celtic teams. If anything, playing in the shadow of the Lions must be daunting. How does any Celtic player match that achievement today? Fortunately for us fans, being brought up on stories of the Lions doesn't mean we don't still fill with overwhelming joy at the thought of the latest triumph.

As a boy growing up through the 1980s and 1990s, while I may not remember the centenary season or the 1989 Scottish Cup final, I do remember being delighted at John Collins lifting the Tennents Sixes trophy. While that six-a-side tournament victory is hardly on the same par as the European Cup 25 years earlier, it came at a time when Celtic didn't win anything and so it meant something to me. It was a night to forget everything else and just enjoy that winning feeling for once.

That's something that can be all too easy to take for granted. It took us ten years to get the league championship back. Since I don't remember the centenary season, that 1998 triumph was my first real memory of Celtic being champions of Scotland. On top of the relief at stopping the ten, that means a lot. I may never celebrate another championship like that and something drastic would need to happen for another league title to mean as much. Regardless, in these ever increasingly televised fixture days I may never have to celebrate another league title listening on the radio.

When Martin O'Neill's side clinched the second part of their treble three years later against St Mirren, I was watching on at home. While that was still better than listening intently to the radio, I still felt distant from the celebrations. But while in 1998 we got the trophy after the match, winning the title in 2001 early meant a wait until the next home match. I was fortunate enough to be in the stadium for that match against Hearts when we got the trophy and that is something I will never forget. It was my first sight of silverware in person, and it wouldn't be my last.

Indeed, since that day in 2001 I've managed to be there for them all. I was there for Livingston in 2002 when they gave us the trophy on the same day we clinched the title, I was in Kilmarnock for the clincher in 2004 and the unusual defeat to Dunfermline on the day we got the trophy at home. I saw us beat Hearts to win the league in 2006 and was there for the draw with Hibernian when we got that trophy, too. I was back in Kilmarnock for Nakamura's late clincher in 2007 and for yet another title party spoiling defeat at home against Hearts after it.

Then of course came to 2008. It may have been different reasons, but victory in 2008 felt just as important as it did in 1998. Not because it would be our first three in a row since the days of Jock Stein, not because we had to stop Rangers, but purely because we had to win it for Tommy. I was at Tannadice that night and although Aberdeen helped the cause I got to be "the guy with the radio" that relayed the news to the rest of the support. The Bhoys on the park did their job, too. I don't think there was every any doubt that night would end any other way.

All of these games are important to me and I can practically rhyme them off the top of my head. Usually more the clinching days than the trophy days - it's easier to remember the games where you win after all. Nevertheless, these days cannot be taken for granted, no matter how big or small the challenge. Celtic have won 44 titles and I can distinctly remember winning 9 of them now, including the most recent two. That's nine magical days in my own life, each with special memories.

The trophy presentation days themselves have, sadly, turned into something of a circus. In fact, against Hearts in 2012 there actually WAS a circus at one point. The victory at Kilmarnock, the third time in eight years I had been down there to watch us clinch the title, felt more important. It was the same in 2013. Although we got the trophy with a victory over St Johnstone, it was clinching the title against Inverness that felt more important.

The carnival that goes with the trophy presentation days is almost taking the shine off them, which is a shame because these are the days that should be celebrated. These are the days that the players work so hard to reach. These are the days we supporters hope for the rest of the season. These are the days that are few and far between. These are the days that make all the other days worthwhile.

Those few victorious days should all be cherished and celebrated when they come round. For the rest of those 45,654 days we've thought about Celtic, or talked about Celtic with our friends, or watched Celtic play opposition from the smallest to the biggest. We live it, we breathe it, we feel it. When we achieve something, we've earned the right to celebrate it and enjoy it to the fullest.

Maybe I feel so strongly about this because I grew up through a barren spell surrounded by Rangers supporters who never let me forget it. My memories of Celtic only reach clarity in the summer of 1989 and, barring that Tennents Sixes victory, it was six years later before I saw us lift anything. That's a long time in the history of Celtic, longer still when you're just a kid.

Or maybe it's because one of my strongest memories from the trip to Seville was standing in a bar just days after that final watching Ceefax tell me the scores on the final day of the league season. We didn't celebrate that day. Maybe it's because I was at Fir Park in 2005. We didn't celebrate that day either. Hell, there are no words to describe how we felt after that. The simple fact is; the bad days always leave scars whether you like it or not, so the good days should never be allowed to pass you by.

So next time there's a title to be celebrated or a cup final victory to be enjoyed, remember how many days there were before it. The days that got you to this point where you thought about victory or worried that it wouldn't come. Remember those scars, the titles we didn't win and the cup finals we lost or didn't even reach. Make the most of those few days of triumph.

And that, your honour, is why I kissed the guy next to me when Joe Ledley scored the third against Hibernian in the Scottish Cup Final!

Crack

Tom Leonard

cuts inty thi box

croass cumzthi centre hoff

a right big animull

crack

doon goes Dalgleesh

ref waves play on

nay penahlti

so McNeil complainzty im

oot cumzthi book

tipicl

wan mair upfurthi luj

Lubo's Fate

Jim McGinley

"Has he gone, Jock?"

"Yes, there was no persuading him."

"Right. Well I just hope he's sure about what he's doing, and the potential consequences. Bloody hell...... this could be a real problem down the line if he digs his heels."

"He says he'll be back tomorrow. You never know, it may all come to nothing."

"But what if it does? What if he comes back and says, "Right, he wants a deal" and wants us to make it formal and start the wheels in motion? Do we really want that?"

"Well, technically in this sort of thing he is the boss."

"Yes I know that, but I have a position to think about too, and the final say on where we spend our money, and I am not at all sure about this. This is a personal crusade if you ask me, and I am wary..... very, very, wary. We could get slaughtered for this...... even by our own people. And in many ways we can't afford that."

"At the same time, the man has a job to do and was entrusted with that job. Should we not let him do it? Should we not put our trust in him and his judgement?"

"Yes we should.... But as part of a team, not as a one man committee making decisions based on the past and some romantic notion in his head. We must consider finance, PR, and the net result on the rest of the team. As a business we are behind in the race and can only take steps that move us forward.... This seems a trip to the past and I am very wary."

"Look on the bright side, he's gone on a twenty four hour trip, will be back tomorrow and, at this moment in time, making a private trip no one knows about. He's not even officially there on our behalf. If it comes to nothing, no one need find out. If he comes back with a positive we can then sit down as a team and analyse the pros and cons and decide from there."

"I suppose so.... But if he comes back with a positive he'll want to proceed, and I might have to stand in his way. That could lead to another problem altogether."

"Jock—you're getting ahead of yourself. Just wait till tomorrow and see what it brings. In the interim we should try to find out more about this guy. Maybe Josef is on to something."

"But if that were so, why would nobody else think the same way? Why would we not know more about him? It's not as if we don't have our ear to the ground with contacts here, there and everywhere. None of those contacts showed the slightest interest here. Not even a mention. Yet here we are discussing the possibility........"

The room door opened and the two men were suddenly faced with a third man entering. He was younger than the two seated men, dressed in a track suit and had a towel over his shoulder.

"Sorry, I was looking for the boss?" said the younger man.

"Well, he's gone for the day, Eric," said Jock.

"For the day?"

"Yes, he will be back tomorrow."

"Where has he gone? Is everything alright?"

"Yes, yes. He's gone abroad for the day—to see a friend."

"To see a friend? ...for the day?"

The two older men looked at one another and, with a nod of agreement, decided to tell Eric more.

"He's gone to meet someone with a view to persuading him to perhaps join us... though, at this stage, we're not sure if the trip will be successful," said Jock.

"……. And we are not at all sure we want him to be successful to be honest. This may prove to be very delicate as we could be in for some…….. conflict."

"Ah," said Eric. "I see. Can I ask who he's gone to meet?"

The older men looked at one another again, before one slid a manila folder across the table. Eric sat down, opened the folder and saw a name and a photograph,

Without delving into the folder any further he looked up at the two men who were watching him closely for any reaction.

He smiled slightly and held up the photograph. "Him?"

Both men nodded.

"You've got to be kidding….. Right?"

The hotel was no different to many of the international hotels the man had visited over many years: modern, luxurious, all the necessary facilities and close enough to the airport to be convenient.

He had personally made the call to set up the meeting even though he knew that, in the strictest sense of the word, it wasn't the way business was usually done. But he considered it a risk worth taking. All he had to do now was convince his target that the proposal would be mutually beneficial, was a good deal and a good move.

Only if he succeeded would the executive-types swing into action with the formal arrangements. That was their world not his. But this was not an executive-type meeting. This was no more than a chat between two old friends. However, as he sat waiting, he pondered how to achieve his intended goal. Although he had known his prey for years, knew him really well…he wasn't sure if that made the forthcoming conversation easier or considerably more difficult.

While waiting in the hotel lobby his mind drifted to Anton. Dear Anton. It was almost two years since all the old gang turned up to see him laid to rest.

He could see him in his mind's eye..... Young Anton.... swarthy.... swashbuckling..... funny..... brave.... in the dressing room pulling on his socks, chatting away, joking and laughing. He missed Anton.... missed talking and listening to him.

His attention turned back to the meeting and he felt an unexplained nervousness. No matter how much he tried to convince himself, he feared revealing a part of himself kept hidden for years in order to gain the trust of the younger man. What if it backfired? What if the younger man concluded that his old friend had finally grown too old for the real world and had lost his marbles entirely?

Just then Lubomir Moravcik came through the door. Small, diminutive, and with an impish grin he'd driven at speed the short distance from Duisburg to Dusseldorf to meet Josef Venglos. Lubomir still looked like a schoolboy in Josef's eyes. Yet he knew he was thirty three years old and, in the eyes of the footballing world, a veteran.

The two men hugged and embraced as only old friends do and, after some brief pleasantries, retired to a private waiting room. Once privacy was assured they asked about one another's families and talked of old times and acquaintances, before Moravcik brought up the business in hand.

"So– you are now in Glasgow– Scotland? And managing Celtic Glasgow?

"Yes Lubomir, that I am."

"And you want me to go there too– at my age?"

"Yes, I do– very much so."

"Boss, I am not at my fittest and cannot hold down a place with Duisburg. My time in the footballing light has come and gone I'm afraid, and as much as I would like to play forever I must listen to Mother Nature telling me it is time to move on in life. Maybe coaching back in Slovakia, maybe somewhere in France."

Josef sighed, poured water into a glass, and looked at his countryman.

"Lubomir, I know how old you are. I know where you have played, how often you have played and for whom you have played. I first saw you as a schoolboy and know fine well that here in Germany you are not the youngest in your current squad. But, I also know that you can do a job for Celtic, even if you do not play the full 90 minutes of each game. This will be good for you, Lubomir– I promise you– and besides, it will stand you in good stead for when you do finally hang up your boots. I have every confidence."

"But Scotland, boss? It is a very different standard to here in the Bundesliga. It is also different to France and St Etienne, and whilst everyone in Europe knows the Celtic of old– with no disrespect they are no longer amongst the big teams of Europe. I tell you, if it is a physical league– requiring fitness and physicality– then I don't feel I am up to it. I know Duisburg see me as surplus. But I can see out my time here, make contacts on mainland Europe and plan for the future. In Scotland? Well I know no one– and no one knows me. I may find myself in a wilderness and miss out on chances here– chances off the park and away from the game– I am not certain at all. Besides, I do not speak a word of English... not one. On the continent I can communicate... French, Slovak, Croatian, German... etc. English? I have nothing... And Scottish English? Ha! I haven't a clue!"

The two friends smiled and talked back and forward.

Venglos briefly outlined how he found the club and the squad. He kept repeating how confident he was that whilst Rangers were the dominant team in Scotland - despite Celtic winning the league the year before - he knew the day would come when they would be toppled from the top of the Scottish tree, and how he believed Moravcik could play a part in that process.

Despite their friendship, Lubomir remained dubious and unconvinced.

Ultimately, Josef knew he would have to take the risk that might jeopardise their long-held friendship.

"Lubomir, do you remember when you first came to Prague?"

"Eh? Yes– I was maybe fifteen or sixteen."

"I was younger– maybe ten years old."

"Why do you ask?"

"Lubomir, I am going to tell you something that you may find hard to believe. Something many might consider strange. Please hear me out as I thought long and hard about telling you this. At the end I will ask you one question and, no matter how you answer, I will respect your decision."

Lubomir looked perplexed but out of respect for his older friend simply nodded his assent.

Josef sat back in his chair and continued – "As you know I was born in Ruzomberok in Slovakia. Until 1918 the town was in Hungary– all mountains, streams and cotton mills. I was never anywhere near Prague until I went with my school not long after the end of the second world war– 1946. I was ten years old and all I wanted to do was play football– football, football, football– that was all I cared about. That visit has stayed with me ever since– though I have often been too embarrassed to speak of it in case people think me a fool.

During that trip to Prague the school team played in a mini tournament held in the Letenske Sady Park. We were not very good I'm afraid but we played a number of games all the same.

The last of our games was watched by a few spectators, one of whom was a very animated old man in a wheel chair. The nurse with him kept telling him to be quiet, but despite this, he continued to shout instructions at us boys. The instructions were in broken Czech and were barked. He seemed angry and spoke in a funny accent– yet he also seemed knowledgeable about football. At the end we were taken over by our coach to meet him. Apparently he was quite famous– or indeed had been at one time.

He was introduced as Dedek and was eighty years old. We were told he was the Grandpa of Czech Football, had been the manager of Slavia Prague for twenty five years and won many championships, including what is regarded as the forerunner of the European Cup. He coached in a different way to anything ever seen. He knew about tactics, and muscles and physiotherapy long before anyone else. He was a national hero and helped coach the most successful national teams, at the Olympics and in the lead-up to the World Cup. We hung on his every word.

However, the strangest thing about Dedek was revealed in a ten minute story. For despite being a hero in Czechoslovakia, he was born in Scotland– in a town called Dumbarton. He was a riveter in a ship yard, played football part-time for the local club and gained success getting to the Scottish Cup Final in 1887. Then he said everything changed– changed in a way he could never imagine, and a way you may never believe.

In 1888 he was asked to turn out as a guest for a new team– a club to be called Celtic in Glasgow. There had been several attempts to start a club called Celtic and they had all failed. He was reluctant at first but eventually agreed, though he honestly felt this club would fail too. So– on the 28th of May 1888– Dedek took his position as Celtic's first centre forward and, when taking their first kick-off, became the very first player to touch a ball for Celtic Glasgow. He started the whole Celtic ball rolling– literally. They played against a team called Rangers Swifts and won 5-2.

After the game Dedek attended the celebration party and he was asked to join Celtic permanently, but said no.

He returned to play for Dumbarton; a good team then and about 25 miles from Glasgow– but try as he might he could not get the Celtic thing out of his head. Clubs from England continually pursued him but he kept bumping into two Celtic men called Glass and Maley who promised him that something special would happen to him at Celtic Park– a park the supporters built themselves, Lubo. The way he spoke, it was as if they said Celtic Park had been fashioned out of magic– you know like by a wizard?"

Josef felt his face blush slightly at this talk of wizardry, but Lubo, to his credit, kept a straight face and focused on the old man's eyes.

Josef composed himself and continued: "Eventually Dedek signed for Celtic in August 1889 and stayed until 1897, winning leagues and cups along the way. He was apparently like you, Lubo: an entertainer, good feet, ferocious shot and a crowd pleaser. His nickname was the rooter– because his shots were so hard they uprooted the posts.

After he retired from playing, he went back to working in the shipyards but kept up to date with football. He travelled, and in 1905 Celtic toured . through Europe and by coincidence came to Prague– by design or accident– Dedek came, too, and somehow got the job of managing Slavia Prague on 15th February 1905– He was a huge success– and he never went back to Scotland.

But on that day in the Letenske he said that his whole life in football truly started that day he turned out for a team called Celtic. As a young boy I listened to this old man in the park and he told us that if you can play football at all then you can play at Celtic Park in Scotland. He said it was a place where, for some, real destiny awaited, and that strange and wonderful things happen. So I always knew about Celtic Park, always believed in the old man's tale that it was a magical place. When I got the chance to go there I didn't hesitate– and I have seen it – seen it with my own eyes– I have seen and felt what the old man told me of– and it exists. It is there and it is real– and most of all it says to me, 'Moravcik! Moravcik' You are the kind of player that can play there, Lubomir– you will shine and achieve things you have never before experienced– believe me.

The old man's real name was Johnny Madden– go look him up– the very first guy to kick a ball for Celtic, Lubo, and he ends up a national hero in our back yard? A guy who was destined to fit rivets in a shipyard all his days– until he went to Celtic park– and I meet him in a public park one tram stop up from the Sparta station in 1946? And he looks into my eyes all those years ago and says if you get the chance one day go to Celtic Park because strange things happen there? And so here I am– all these years later. The manager of the club where that old man kicked the first football, which in turn led him to be a legend in the country that both you and I were born.

So here is my question, Lubomir. I know you have doubts about your fitness and about Scotland. I know you have a future to think of and that you could have gone to Marseilles and Juventus and regretted not making those moves. So trust me, Lubo– just this once more. Will you come with me to have a look at Celtic and their ground? Will you come and *feel* it?

See what the old man said was true all those years ago– and if you don't get that feeling that you can play there, that you won't fit in and that there is not something different about the place– well we will pay all the expenses of your visit and you can come back here– nothing lost at all.

What do you say Lubomir– will you walk through the Parkhead gates with me for a look at the place where Dedek kicked the first ball? I swear you will just never know if you don't!"

"No we are not kidding, that is who Josef has gone to see," said Jock.

"Moravcik?"

"Eh… do I take it from that remark that you have heard of him, Eric?"

"Heard of him? I played against him!"

"Really?"

"Yes. Really!"

"We know nothing about him other than that Josef is away to see him with a view to persuading him to come here. We have doubts and, whilst we don't want a row with Josef when he is so new to the job, we have real concern about this."

"OK, first of all I have to say you appointed Josef, and in my opinion you have to back him in any footballing matter unless the finances prohibit any deal. The boss is the boss and that's the way it should be in any matter."

"Yes, we agree with that, but at the same time we do not have to, -- actually cannot--- sanction the employment of just anyone he throws at us….. Any appointment has to make sense… even if it is someone he knows well from his past and who is a friend."

"But this is Moravcik we're talking about."

"So? All we know is that he is an old protégé of Josef's… they go back years."

"Lubomir Moravcik was possibly the most two-footed player I've ever seen on a football field. With either foot he could more or less make the ball do anything he wanted. He played midfield, or just behind the strikers, and could pass, dribble, cross, shoot... you name it he could do it. He should have been a footballing superstar."

"Well why wasn't he then?"

"I can't answer that. I only saw him up close towards the end of my time at Metz, though I kept an eye on French football and saw how he stood out at St Etienne. He was there for years.... And then he moved on to........ Bastia I think?"

"Why did he never move to a bigger club?"

"I don't know that either.... He could have..... Possibly should have. When I moved back from France I concentrated on other things. But I tell you this: if Josef thinks Moravcik would be a good addition to the staff here then I'd follow that instinct. If we could harness his knowledge and skill he could teach the players all sorts of techniques and movement. He'd be a great addition to the coaching staff in my opinion."

The other two men in the room looked at one another briefly.

"Josef doesn't want him to come and coach..... he wants him to play."

"What?"

"You heard... he wants him to play."

Eric quickly reached for the file again and opened it. "He is less than two years younger than me. He will be 34 next summer."

"Yes we know."

Eric Black got up from the table and walked to a nearby window and looked out. "He wants him to play....to the end of the season?"

"The way he's talking he wants to offer him a contract for a couple of years. Effectively he wants to sign someone in his mid-thirties who most people will never have heard of. We'll get slaughtered in the press. They'll

28

have our guts for garters..... and unless the guy turns out to be a superstar... which is very unlikely.... the fans will go ballistic."

"But that's just it.... Moravcik IS a superstar.... He's just a superstar that people don't know. But Josef knows it. The only question is can he still play?"

"Well that's the point.... he can't even get a game for Duisburg in the Bundesliga, so why does Josef think he could play in the Scottish league for us and do a job?"

"You'll have to ask him that, but..... and you say they go back a long way.... if there is any way that Josef can get Moravcik to play then, honestly, it may a masterstroke. He is a creative genius with a football..... bloody hell..... the fans will love him.... absolutely love him.... if he can still play."

"Anyway that's where Josef is..... and depending on how he gets on we may have to sanction his transfer..... or risk coming into conflict with Josef.... which we obviously don't want."

"I am going to say it again. Josef is the boss in football matters. You gave him the job so you should back his judgement....... And maybe.... just maybe..... you should back his hunches if this is a hunch."

"What would you do? Honestly. Can a thirty something unknown European really come and make a difference here in this league?"

Eric paused before replying.

"Well, I've gotten to know Josef Venglos reasonably well. He's a man who believes in skill and people, in methodology and science, and at the same time believes...... that there is something special about Celtic among football clubs. I don't know where that comes from or why it should be.... He hasn't told me.... But he has said that fate led him here for a purpose and to do a job. If he believes Moravcik can play here then you have to back his judgement. And if Moravcik is fit and can pass a medical Celtic Park will never have seen anyone like him"

Lubomir Moravcik looked across the room at Josef Venglos and said:

"I still don't know, boss. That is a nice story but..... just a story after all, and I am not sure I can plan my future on a story.... Even a story told by you. I have always held you in high regard. You have always been there for me to call... with Nitra, in France, with Czechoslovakia and with Slovakia.... But this is different. I now have to look at earning a living.... Looking after my family....... Without kicking a football. It is time to take the step that you took, boss. Move away from playing, and move on to coaching. If I come to Scotland and play for a year or so how will that advance my chances of coaching? Let's face it I can't coach in Scotland or England..... I don't have the language. But I can coach in Europe.... It is something that I really need to consider. Of course I would love to play and keep playing but how realistic is that?

"Lubomir, you are correct. The story of Mr Madden is a good story... a nice story.... But also a story with a point and poignancy, and with respect, so far you have only heard half the tale and why I consider the story as more than just a story, and something which points to sheer pragmatism..... nothing more and nothing less."

Moravcik looked back across the room and raised his eyebrows, shrugged his shoulders, smiled and said, "You know I will always listen, boss. If you have something to say just say it no matter what.... I will consider anything you have to say."

"Lubomir, you know that I spent my entire playing career with Slovan Bratislava?"

"Yes."

"We had a good team. Not a great team, but a good team.... A team to build upon and take forward. We were Czech then...... although we were also Slovaks and very proud to be looked upon as Slovaks and a Slovakian team first and foremost. You yourself were the only Slovak in a very good Czech team."

"Yes I know.... I was very conscious of that."

"I had to give up my playing days when I contracted hepatitis..... so my playing career ended early and my coaching career began as a result. Perhaps, because of that, I have always had a tendency to look forward and back at the same time."

"How do you mean--- look forward and look back? I don't think I understand?"

"What I mean, Lubomir is that I look at football today and learn things from the past. When you are playing, you only look at now, the game in hand, the game you are playing. Yes, you might consider a career move where you will play for the next couple of seasons and so on, but it is all very current.... very now.

When, like me, you are forced to stop playing early, you look at what happened to you, what influenced you at the time, even though you perhaps didn't know it at the time. Plus, when I went into coaching I wanted to find out what made the footballer—what made him run faster, jump higher and so on and so forth. I gained qualifications and learned about sports medicine, physicality, training regimes, diet – all the things that make a good player a better player."

"Forgive me, boss, but you are losing me--- what has all this to do with me going to Celtic? What has it to do with the old man in Letenske Park?"

"It has EVERYTHING to do with that old man and that conversation, Lubomir... absolutely everything!"

"How boss—I don't understand."

"Well, remember he told me that everything changed for him when he signed for the new team called Celtic?"

"Yes."

"Well by the time he came to Prague he knew all about physiotherapy, being fit, tactics, coaching."

"Yes."

"But he also talked of..... spirit.... That certain something you can't touch but which changes the way you play.... changes your life..... changes everything.....

Many call it fate, Lubomir..... Some say destiny, or luck or whatever. Others might call it belief...... belief that they have somehow found their destiny or fate and that from there and then on..... things will be different. However, fate and destiny and luck can be helped along.... Fate can be moulded with the right people in the right place at the right time. Celtic park is the right place, and this is your time, and that I know for a fact.... It is not a dream or a nice story or an old man's daft notion. It is a fact. And I know, not because the old man told me but because I saw it for myself, and today I still see it...... Your destiny, or at least part of it, awaits you at Celtic park because I know your personality..... and you will respond to the spirit of the place..... You will play for longer and go further than you thought possible. I am sure of it."

"Are you telling me all this, and talking about fate and luck all because you can tell me my footballing future having taken the job at Celtic park for..... for literally a number of weeks? That is hard to accept, Josef?"

"No, Lubomir.... These last few months only confirmed what I already knew for decades."

"Okay, what did you know for decades?"

"I knew Celtic Park was a place where a reasonable footballer could become good and a good footballer could become great. I can feel it now too. The place is inspiring, it has an atmosphere all of its own... a spirit.... a something I cannot properly name or adequately describe, but I know is there. You won't find it in manuals or see slides of it on sports science courses, but it is there..... it is what the old man said--- a place where, for the select few, things change, confidence grows, and what seemed impossible or unlikely comes to be."

"And you have known this for decades.....from talking to an old man in a park?"

"No, Lubomir, the old man only told me about Celtic Park. I saw it for myself thirty five years ago!"

"What?"

"My recent appointment did not bring about my first visit to Celtic Park. I first went there in the early sixties."

"You played there?"

"No, Lubomir, that is just it, I did not play there."

"Sorry, but you are losing me, boss."

"Slovan Bratislava played at Celtic Park in the European Cup Winners Cup in late February 1964, Lubomir. Injury prevented me playing so instead I sat in the stand that night....... with my close friend and your namesake...... Anton Moravcik."

"Anton? He wasn't playing either?"

"No, Lubomir, both of us missed out playing in Glasgow. My place was taken by Alexander Hovarth."

"Hovarth?"

"Yes, Lubo, Hovarth. The previous year we had been drawn against Tottenham Hotspur at the same stage of the European Cup Winners Cup. Anton and I both played in the home tie against these great Tottenham players—Greaves, White, McKay and many others. On our own ground we beat them 2-0, but it was an ugly, dirty game in front of a crowd of 17,000 or so. The return leg was even worse – before a hostile London crowd – we lost 6-0 and went out. It was a really nasty, bad tempered affair and the packed White Hart Lane had a very poisonous feel about it—and I am not saying that because we lost. The atmosphere was still ugly even when they were winning the tie. Maybe it was because we were viewed as "Eastern Bloc" players from behind the Iron Curtain, I don't know—but it was not enjoyable, it was not a good place to play football."

"Okay."

"One year later we drew Celtic. At the time they did not have famous players. Most of our team knew nothing about them really, and so they thought the game was likely to be more of the same from a British side --- physical, bad-tempered football with an ugly, bad-humoured home crowd.

Then, I told the story about my meeting Dedek and what he told me about being the first to kick a football for Celtic. To be honest, most had the same reaction as you—it is a good story, Josef, but let's get back to the real world.

However, one or two asked a little more about the story.... And one of those was Anton. What a player he was, Lubomir.... Far better than me... much more clever... like you. Twenty five caps, Lubomir..... he appeared twenty five times for Czechoslovakia and scored ten times.... Not bad for a midfielder eh?"

"Not Bad at all, boss."

"What a pair he and Masopust were in the middle of the park --- and you should hear Masopust about Celtic? Anyway, although Anton and I were both disappointed to be left out in Glasgow we watched from the stand...... and there it was, Lubomir.... Celtic Park. Not quite the way it was when Madden played, but very different to today."

"How so, Josef?"

"Well today there is a modern stadium with a huge stand facing you when you come out of the tunnel--- as good as any in Europe. Then, it was more old-fashioned with lower buildings. But it was not the buildings, Lubomir, it was...... the atmosphere.... the feel of the place....... the spirit. It almost talked to you.... although I know that sounds daft. During the game I had experienced nothing like it..... nothing whatsoever."

"What do you mean?"

"Against Tottenham, the atmosphere was poisonous. Against Celtic on a cold February night a crowd of 55,000 came to see their team play us and the atmosphere was spectacular. Like a carnival. They sang and sang. They cheered. They shouted and waved their hats in the air as the game went back and forward—and the game did go back and forward. The best two players on the park were the goalkeepers—theirs was called Fallon and we had the marvellous Viliam Schrojf who had one of his best games ever.

The point is this game was nothing like Tottenham—this was an open game--- with end to end play. Little did we know at the time but their players would shortly become famous around the globe—McNeill, Clark, Johnstone, Murdoch, Chalmers and so on, but that night we played well—really well. It was a great game to watch, Lubomir, but all the while I sat in the stand with Anton and he kept saying, "I wish I was playing...I wish I was playing." So did I. We both wanted to play in that atmosphere—we could feel it, taste it, touch it. And what an effect it had on the Celtic players. By the end of the game they ran, jumped and tackled as if the game had just started. They were just unbelievable. The whole thing was unbelievable.

In the end we lost to a penalty goal, but were confident of getting a result in Bratislava. However, at the end of the game, the crowd cheered and clapped us. We hadn't seen that before. In the stand people shook our hand, and afterwards we were made most welcome by the Celtic people. Afterwards, with the help of an interpreter, we got speaking to some of their players and they made it plain that they played for that crowd, for their fans, and that made a difference to them. I didn't tell anyone the Madden story that night for fear they would laugh, but I later regretted that, and for years now I wish I had.

In the return leg, try as we did, and even with Anton playing, we could not beat Celtic. We lost 1-0 again in our own stadium, and once again after the game we were told that these Glasgow players play for their fans.... Play for...... something I cannot quite put my finger on and which can't be found in any manual.

So that was my first experience of Celtic Park, Lubo and it confirmed all I was told.... It is a magical place.... A place for footballers—real footballers--- and where some will fulfil their destiny just like Dedek said.

Within a couple of years Anton and I retired from the game, but he always talked about the visit to Celtic park— about the atmosphere and how it made their players run and tackle and play as if by magic. He said that sitting there watching was quite magic in itself.

But that is not what sealed my belief in Celtic Park. Within three years or so, many of that Celtic team went on to beat Inter Milan in the 1967 European Cup Final in Lisbon. They played beautiful flowing football. They attacked and moved the ball and the opposition about in a way that was fantastic, and this was against the great Inter side of Herrera who had dominated Europe by getting in front and killing the game stone dead. We did not see that game immediately of course as there was no live television available to us, but we did get to see it eventually. I watched it with Anton and he raved about Celtic, the movement, the passing, the formation.... And we talked about what the old man had said....... For some, their real destiny will only be found at Celtic Park.

Their manager that day was Jock Stein, Lubomir. Someone, like me, whose playing career ended early due to injury. Someone who thought about the game, about the way it is played, and he too talked about the magic of the place..... Something about how men grow to fit that shirt they play in.... how they change. He talked in the same language as Dedek..... but he was not an old man in a park; he was the man who had just led a team to victory over Herrera's Inter. This was real... all very real.... but still the stuff of folklore and fairy-tales.

Two years later, Slovan Bratislava had their greatest moment when Alex— Alexander Hovarth lead them to victory against Herrera's old team in the European Cup Winners Cup. No one fancied us to beat Barcelona but sure enough we did.

I mention that because, as you know, Anton passed away two years ago. I went to his funeral and all the old guard were there including Alex. We talked about Anton and reminisced and so on but while we were there Alex told me that Anton came to believe in my story about the old man in Letenske Sady Park. Anton and he talked to one another about that night in Glasgow and how Anton wished he had been playing.

In turn, Alex also told me he believed he learned something that night out on the Celtic turf. He could see in the eyes of his opponents that they had a determination, a zest and a belief that came from the crowd—like a drug or a potion. Alex said that had it not been for that night at Celtic Park he would not have become the player he did, and that were it not for that night and some of the things the trip to Celtic Park instilled in Alex and others,

Slovan would never have won the Cup Winners Cup five years later---
because he and others not only felt that special atmosphere, they also
learned something. Remember, they played really well at Celtic park....
They enjoyed the experience and built on it. Yes, mostly different players,
but enough stayed to talk about belief, and what can be achieved if you
play for a cause as opposed to playing for the sake of competition.

So Lubomir, now a great big modern stadium stands proud in Glasgow, but
that atmosphere is still there. It has a motivation all of its own. I can't
define it in terms of science and there is no mathematical equation or
formula to help reproduce it. You will only find it if you see for yourself,
but I assure you it is there. For you, Lubomir, it will be like being the only
Slovak in a Czech team.... It will make you want to burst with pride and
passion. You and Celtic are a fit, Lubomir, but I have no diagrams or
scientific charts to prove it. I only have the story of the old man in the park,
and the memories of myself and Anton... and belief in magic. I have
nothing more.

It is up to you if you want to come but I say again, I look at the squad, and
the stadium and it all says to me "Moravcik, Moravcik" but this time it is
not Anton, it is Lubomir that it calls out for... and this time in a green and
white hooped shirt."

Lubomir Moravcik looked at his mentor and, after a pause, finally asked:

"Boss, is there anyone else at the club you have talked to about this?
Anyone who.... honestly feels the same "thing" that you do..... that
somehow fate will call on them at Celtic park? It is a great story, but if
what you say is true, surely someone else there would feel the same way?"

"Yes Lubomir. If you come and have a look, speak to the players and
backroom staff. Speak to whoever you want; ask them how they find it
there. You can have free access to help you decide. Of course, there will be
language barriers, but we have a multilingual squad, and French speakers
and all sorts of different languages, but you will be able to talk to them,
and I can get an interpreter.......... Oh........ and I suggest you somehow
have a chat with Henrik Larsson."

A few weeks later Dr Venglos sat in his office considering his options when there was a knock at the door.

"Can I come in, boss?"

"Yes Lubomir."

"Boss, I don't know your plans, but I want to play tomorrow. I want to face Rangers."

"Are you fit, though, Lubo. You have been here only two short weeks and I recall you telling me in Dusseldorf that if it was a physical league and a physical challenge then you felt that you were not up to the challenge. This will be a physical game and maybe it is better if you allow one of the younger players to start...."

"No. I want to play..... from the start!"

"I see..... well, I will think about it..... I obviously need to put out my strongest team...."

"Boss. You told me about this place. You told me about Celtic Park and all its magic. Well now I have seen it and, to be honest, I have felt it. I feel I can play here. I feel I have to play here.... for these people. There were 58,000 here for Dundee two weeks ago. It was a great atmosphere, but it will be better with Rangers as the visitors, it will be a big game.... I want to play... for them.... for you....and for Anton.... for Anton Moravcik who never got to play here."

Venglos merely nodded

The normally smiling Moravcik seemed serious and almost angry. "And there is something else."

"What?"

"As you know, I have no English, but I am not a stupid man. I may not be able to read what the press have been saying in the papers but I know they have ridiculed you, ridiculed the club, and ridiculed me in signing for

Celtic. I am the cheap option instead of getting a real player, apparently. I am the old man; the unknown has been so to speak. Is that not correct?"

"Well, Lubomir, there has been some talk like that but ignore it; it is the chatter of fools."

"No, I don't want to ignore it, and if you let me play against Rangers I will talk to the press and put the record straight. I will talk to the Celtic support and show them the truth and explain why you have faith in me and why I have faith in you, and this club and your old man's story."

There was no sign of the impish grin that usually adorned the face of Lubomir Moravcik and Josef Venglos could see that he was deadly serious. Partly to humour his countryman, Venglos said simply, "Okay Lubomir, I will have an interpreter standing by, and if things go well maybe you can say a few.... well-chosen words to the press."

Instantly, the impish grin returned to Lubo Moravcik's face. "Oh that will not be necessary, Josef. I have my own interpreter."

Venglos looked puzzled. "You do?"

"Yes boss, I will not need an interpreter...... I am going to talk in the language I know best..... I am going to make the ball talk.......... for me and for you and for all the Celtic fans...... for Anton and for Dedek..... If you can play football you can play here and tomorrow is my chance. I will make the ball talk for me, boss. It can't be misquoted or misinterpreted but in reality I will not utter a single word..... None will be needed."

And with that Lubomir Moravcik left Josef Venglos with his thoughts....... and the story he first heard from an old man in Prague that for some their true fate would only be realised at Celtic Park, Glasgow.

The First Thing The Huns Saw

Paul Larkin

We all have people we look up to. There are varying reasons as to why we look up to other individuals, mostly personal ones. One of the people I looked up to, and still remember every day, is Gabriel Patrick Quinn.

Gabriel was born in Townhead, Glasgow on St Patrick's Day 1924. He married Mary and had nine children. A hard-working man who liked to relax watching his favourite football team in Glasgow's East End.

In 1939 when Hitler's fascists began to overrun Europe in their quest for world domination Gabriel didn't hesitate when conscripted for the war effort. Gabriel found himself in Troop 303 Battery, Assault Div., The 3rd British Infantry.

After years of loss on all sides, the big move was on, June 6th 1944, D-Day.

150,000 Allied troops landed along a 50-mile stretch of heavily-fortified French coastline to fight Nazi Germany on the beaches of Normandy, France. General Dwight D. Eisenhower called the operation a crusade in which "we will accept nothing less than full victory". More than 5,000 ships and 11,000 aircraft supported the invasion, and by day's end, the Allies gained a foot-hold in France. The D-Day cost was high with more than 9,000 Allied soldiers killed or wounded as the march across Europe to defeat Hitler began.

One of the men involved in those historic beach landings was Gabriel Patrick Quinn. I say "involved", but that's not nearly a strong enough word and doesn't do the man justice. Gabriel was at the spearhead of the attack in the first Bren Gun Carrier that landed on Sword Beach, Normandy.

During last minute preparations Gabriel was waterproofing his tank with putty. After finishing he realised he had some left so he stepped back and thought for a few seconds. Moving around to the front of his tank he wrote in big, bold letters: GLASGOW CELTIC.

And so when his vehicle raced ashore, amid the German bombs and bullets raining down, the first words the Huns saw was GLASGOW CELTIC.

After the battle to conquer the beach a jubilant and grateful Gabriel stopped his Bren Gun Carrier briefly to check for any damage to his vehicle or artwork when a Sherman Tank right in front of him took a direct hit.

Gabriel swore to his dying day, which came in 2002, that it was either the luck of the Irish or "GLASGOW CELTIC" that saved him.

There is an afterthought to this story. One of Gabriel's best pals was a Catholic from the Falls Road, James Joseph Magennis. Although Gabriel was conscripted at 18, there was no conscript in the north of Ireland and it has to be said that it was mostly Protestants who joined up.

His friend would be the only winner of a Victoria Cross from Ireland. Sadly, on his return, Belfast dignitaries snubbed John and he could not get work anywhere. He ended up selling his V.C. for £70 and going to England to find work.

He died in 1986 in England and it was only years after this that Belfast began to honour him.

Perceptions of Paradise

J J Whelan

Pre-match rain comes pouring down

We make our way to the holy ground

Floodlit stars light up the pitch

Turns glistening rain to crystal tips

Winter wind whips o'er our face

Ourselves alone in this wondrous place

The Spirit is high as tis' our mood

Fortune changed from bad to good

We hear the chants from up above

Songs of history, of the club we love

Sung with passion and with pride

Our Heritage we shall not hide

Gone the Jungle and its classic roar

93,000 fans we'll see no more

No spearmint chewing gum or macaroon

No standing room or greasy spoon

The Ultras and the Green Brigade

Their endless banners being displayed

Our shiny seats are somewhat chic

Fancy concourse with merchandise boutique

The full facade may have changed

But our history will long remain

With this reflection of long ago

It's still Paradise to which we go.....

Trip to Lisbon

Dutchbhoy

Cascais is an idyllic coastal settlement just along the coast from the Portuguese capital of Lisbon where Celtic conquered Europe. Being so close I know this is my lifetime chance of visiting the ground in which that historic game was played. I assume the stadium must be in the city centre but I check first with my new friend, Joao, the man at the hotel desk, who speaks excellent English. I thought he'd be a Benfica fan but, much to my pleasure, he's a Sporting Lisbon fan. Any man, whatever his background, must be alright if his chosen team plays in green and white hoops.

As if that isn't enough our budding friendship was given an extra boost by the fact Graeme Souness is manager of Benfica. How the mighty have fallen. A team once graced with the likes of Eusebio, Torres and Colunha now under the tutelage of a barbarous hun. Joao tells me there are already loud murmurings of discontent among the Benfica faithful.

To my surprise and dismay, Joao informs me the original Stadium of Light is not actually in Lisbon. My initial sadness is soon overturned when he reveals it's only a fifteen- minute train ride from where we're standing.

I say goodbye and head to the small station in Cascais. Within minutes I'm on the train to Lisbon. It's a short journey to the designated station. I expected a large train concourse and infrastructure suggesting a nearby magnificent stadium. What I get is a tiny hut, a few houses and a large forest. For a minute I think I've got off at the wrong station, or that maybe Joao was really a hun in disguise.

There's an old man sweeping up leaves with a broom outside the station. I approach him and say, 'Estadio?'

He looks at me and walks away.

I think my sheer bulk might have frightened the poor wee man. However, after a few minutes he reappears with two young boys with a plastic football, says something to them and points up the hill where the forest is. I thank him and let the laddies lead the way, passing and kicking the ball, occasionally inviting yours-truly to make an arse of himself.

After about ten minutes, with no estadio, in sight I begin to lose heart. To be sure, for a late January day the weather is magnificent. Blue skies, no wind, a bright sun and a temperature which Northern Europeans can only envy at this time of year. The pine forest smells beautiful. On my right, evidence of Portugal's economic renaissance; an ultra- modern shooting range, an equestrian centre, and an American football field. But, worryingly, still no estadio.

I'm looking right downwards into a dip when, almost instinctively, I turn left and there it is before me. Between either side of the forest there's a road leading straight into the stadium. What makes it even stranger is the absence of signs giving any indication that a building of this size and stature is in the vicinity. The two youngsters take off and I give them a wave before making my way to the ground. It seems to rise before me, because the lack of a roof makes it difficult to get any sense of scale. The circular stadium also appears incomplete. There's a huge space I can walk through: no turnstiles, no walls, no barriers, nothing. I remember vaguely that, in 1967, there was a wee makeshift stand erected just for the game to provide VIPs with a bit of shade. This, presumably, is where I'm standing now.

I head towards the end Celtic defended in the second half of the game.

The stadium looks to have been constructed from huge slabs of granite hewn from a nearby quarry. There are no seats. I take my vantage point at the very top of the upper tier and finally appreciate the full panoramic view of the pitch.

What must it have been like for the ordinary Celtic supporters from Scotland? My mind spools back to the grainy black-and-white footage of BBC Scotland showing ordinary Tims crammed into wee cars, dubious buses and fat planes, making tortuous paths to Portugal. Who knows what sacrifices they made to get to Lisbon? From somewhere they found the money, came in droves and showed the world what Celtic football club was all about.

I settle myself down on a granite slab and am transported back to a crowded living room in West Lothian. Watching our recently acquired black and white telly, with the X-shaped- aerial on top, there's a nervous anticipation before the game kicks off. My father's worked all the overtime available on the building site to feed and clothe seven kids, not easy on a labourer's wage. A simple thing like a telly is a great luxury. His Celtic mates from work are here, well-oiled and in fine voice. I love it because I'm the youngest and, as they come in the door, every man gives me a tanner. No women are allowed. My mother and sisters all banished from the hoose for the night. Most of the men are in their late thirties and have been through some tough times following Celtic.

Back in the estadio I'm trying to locate where the key incidents of the game took place. Down to my far right, I see where Jim Craig barged into an Italian and, if I am honest, gifted a daft penalty. I see where Mazzola placed the ball on the penalty spot, walked backwards, completed his run up, and arrogantly stroked the ball into the corner of the net, leaving poor old Ronnie Simpson helpless.

Back in the hoose, I understand why the women folk were asked to leave as the air turns blue. But the game picks up and Celtic, after the early setback, start playing like we know they can. The bhoys quickly pick up the tempo. Bertie and Bobby are running the show, pulling all the strings. The movement of their teammates is phenomenal, with players interchanging and dragging the Italians all over the place. We're peppering their goals with shots from all ranges. The ball just won't go in-- there's always a leg, a foot, a head, a piece of wood and above all, the man in black, Giuliano Sarti. I hadn't heard of this guy before but he's surely having the game of his life.

In my head the half time whistle blows and I decide to change ends. As I walk around, I realise that the pictures are there but there is no sound. Who provided the narrative to Celtic's greatest triumph?

Kenneth Wolstenholme was the man. The previous summer he'd commentated at Wembley on England's World Cup win. Wolstenholme belonged to an era when BBC commentators commented upon what they saw and not what they think they should have seen. There was no denying Wolstenholme's genuine joy for Celtic when they won that day, and, as a boy, it was one of the highlights. It would have been horrendous had one of BBC Scotland's huns been allowed to record our greatest moment for posterity. Almost as bad as the likes of John Motson or Barry Davies who see excellence where mediocrity is staring them in the face. Wolstenholme's commentary was exemplary; the Englishman called it as he saw it.

It dawns on me, as I trek towards the other goal, there's not another single person in the vast amphitheatre. The lack of noise only emphasises what it must have been like on that night. As I sit down on another granite slab behind the opposition goal to watch the second half, I'm back again in the packed living room, which is electric with tension and anticipation.

I'm relegated to the role of nipper boy on the building site and sent, with increasing frequency as the Celtic attacks founder on the edge of Inter's penalty box, to fetch beer bottles from the crates stacked in the kitchen. Beer is in dark, clumsy bottles and requires a lot of effort for a nine-year-old boy to open them without spilling the stuff.

In the second half Celtic pen Inter in, but this isn't a question of the Italians simply sitting back and sucking in the pressure. They can't get out of their half. Sarti's still performing minor miracles but a goal has to come. When it does, it's spectacular. Tommy Gemmell producing the sort of goal fit to win any cup. He's hit the ball so hard I only realise it's a goal when the net bulges. The hoose is in a state of pandemonium, grown men behaving like wee boys. We have them on the turn. The winner comes courtesy of a Stevie Chalmers touch. The final whistle blows and an enormous roar of relief and joy fills the room. I'm thrown into the air and, to add to the pleasure, given more tanners and the occasional half-crown.

I'm down to pitch level and walk on the turf. It's beautiful underfoot and manicured like Wimbledon. I walk round and stand where the key incidents took place, then move to the side-lines and stand where Jock Stein stood all those years ago. For the first time today I begin to feel emotional. Words cannot adequately convey what that man did for Celtic and the debt we owe him. A superb coach, brilliant man-manager and unrivalled tactician but, most importantly, a great man. When Stein spoke people listened. He spoke the common sense of the working man. He was a very intelligent man but, like thousands of other youngsters, forced down the mines to earn a living. I feel a twinge of illogical guilt; a big softy like me allowed the benefit of a university education when the likes of Jock Stein were only granted a basic education. He escaped from the pits to play professional football and manage Celtic, and his heart remained with Celtic even years after his departure. His subsequent treatment by the Celtic Board was one of the most disgraceful chapters in the club's history. What must he have been feeling as the final whistle in the Stadium of Light beckoned? Outwardly quiet and in control, but you can bet that inside his stomach was churning.

I look upwards, towards the winner's podium, and see, captured for eternity, Billy McNeill standing there with cup aloft. Not for nothing was Billy nicknamed Caesar. Tall and erect he stands out above the joyful chaos surrounding him.

At home, I keek out of the living room window, and notice that the greatest moment in Scotland's sporting history passes the other houses in the scheme by. There's an eerie silence and no movement from within any of the other houses.

To hell with them. Celtic against the rest, that's how it always was and always will be. Not paranoia, but a true reflection of society. I don't understand what unites my father and his pals from the building site, but I sense it's more than a game of football. I sense it's about self-respect and feeling valued.

I make my way out of the stadium and head down the path, past the forest towards the station.

I wonder if it was a good idea to come here. It's taken a lot more out of me than I imagined. I've been assailed with images, voices, colours and people from the past. I realise, too, that it isn't just about visiting a football ground, or even replaying the game in my head. It's about people and a way of life gone, never to return.

One of the great things about the Celtic players of that time was they looked and sounded just like us, because they were just like us. They knew what it was to play for Celtic and represent their fans. The new breed of Celtic supporter is certainly wealthier and perhaps in some ways better educated. However, driven by consumerism some have lost the understanding of the emotional involvement that goes with being a Celtic supporter. 'Lisbon', for some, has become a mill-stone that's raised unrealistic expectations. But we shouldn't be looking at it like that. It should be seen for what it was, a wonderful night, in a wonderful place, at a wonderful time. The socio-economic conditions which prevailed after the Second World War no longer exist, and not enough Scottish youngsters play football in the numbers required to provide lasting excellence.

I'm at the station hut again. The auld man is sitting in the shade drinking from a bottle of beer. He motions to me and offers me a bottle (he's obviously got me well weighed-up). I sit down to wait on the train and look up once more towards the forest and imagine droves of ecstatic Tims making their way down towards the wee station. No doubt more than a few spent a peaceful night in the sanctuary of the forest sleeping off huge hangovers. Portugal doesn't plan to use this stadium when hosting forthcoming European Championships. In recent years no major games have been played here. Somehow this seems right. The prospect of renovating, tearing-up and re-building would be an act of sacrilege. This was the right place for the right people. On the face of it you couldn't have got two more differing sets of people than Celtic fans and the many Portuguese who attended the game. But it worked as the reserved Portuguese took to the Celtic fans immediately because of their passion and good humour.

The auld man's been scrutinising me carefully and our eyes meet. "Celtic," he says, and a big smile breaks out on his face.

I nod and he says something I don't understand. I get the feeling the auld man has witnessed this scene many times in the past. Foreigners getting off at his wee station hut and trudging up the path towards the stadium. Separated by language, he's still able to convey to me that he likes Celtic. Maybe he was at the game all those years ago.

I hear the train approach and get up. I shake the auld man's hand and thank him as he shuffles off. With one last look I decide there and then I'll never return to this place. All the images and memories have been exorcised. I don't need to return, I have found Paradise.

The Bowhill Bhoy

John C Traynor

My old dad avowed

(so, it must be true)

that a collier bold,

hale at twenty-two …

who laid down his life

in a daring save

that propelled the lad

to an early grave …

was the best he ever saw.

In the pomp of youth,

strapping … in his prime,

he had talent raw,

in a gift sublime …

a courageous heart

with a reckless edge -

focus, power and grace

to the jersey pledged …

ne'er before or since surpassed.

Meteoric rise,

cruelly brief career -

premature demise,

swathed in grief sincere …

lasting legacy

to both kith and kin

as a treasured son

and a Hoops' linchpin…

now, forever, 'Celtic's John'.

On the fateful day,

in a sick'ning crunch,

consummation sore

of a mother's hunch …

terrors harboured deep

in a Mammy's heart,

lock-fast tight in dread

of his headstrong art …

all unleashed that awful night.

Haunting, lifelong curse

of a young, blond 'bear':

Sam's marauding power,

Johnny's peerless flair …

thitherto unmatched,

thenceforth intertwined

in a dance of death -

to their fates consigned …

one to lore; one, living hell.

As the action froze

in a young mind's eye,

one sharp, piercing scream

rent the Govan sky …

in a grisly trice

two young worlds caved in –

Celtic's prince of gloves

and his 'Micky Finn' …

nascent destiny undone.

If you value life,

as you'll surely do,

then, lament the loss

of a genius true …

humble son of Fife

noble, proud athlete

Johnny Thomson, dear -

Scotland's gem forfeit …

Celtic's 'Bowhill Bhoy' supreme.

Nae Chance

Peter Mullen

Sitting in the Main Stand at Celtic park is a rare occurrence for an East End ten-year-old boy. This Garngad son, of a Garngad dad, is usually parked next to the big pylon between the Celtic End and the Jungle. Today is an exception to the pylon rule and, due to a mix-up with the ticket allocation for the Millburn Celtic Supporters Club, we're amid the well-to-do and dignitaries. I can see lots of priests, and my dad says there's a couple of Cardinals and actors. There's also a sprinkling of ex-Celtic players and current reserve-team players present at the invitation of the old board.

It takes us ages to reach our seats. My dad seems to know everyone, and they all know him. That's because he goes to all the home games, away games, reserve games, friendlies. If there's a Celtic team playing a kickabout he'll be there. My mum says he spends more time watching Celtic than at home.

Listening to my dad's stories always makes me wish I'd been born earlier so I could've seen the Lisbon Lions play.

We're now at a time when the Lisbon Lions are breaking up. Big Jock has the unenviable task of embarking on a new era and rebuilding a team expected to simply carry on the success of the most famous of teams in Celtic's history. Mind you, I'm sure if anyone can do it, then big Jock's the man.

As usual, the Hoops are running over the top of this Aberdeen side with chances and goals coming from all angles.

During a break in proceedings, my old man points along the row and asks, 'Do you know any of them?'

I glance at the athletic-looking lads barely a half dozen seats away.

I try hard, but with only the Citizen and The Celtic View being the main media channels I'm struggling to name any of the lads. Only one catches my eye. Lou Macari. Wow, I am sitting but a few seats from a star in the making.

'That is the Quality Street Gang,' my dad enthused.

'Ah...right,' I replied in knowing fashion, even though I didn't have a clue what he was on about. Half-time beckoned and this Quality Street Gang began weaving past seat after seat towards me. 'Dad...dad! Look...look,' came out in a hurried, hysterical screech.

One blonde-haired lad, immaculate in what seemed to be the uniform of these lads - a beige Gabardine coat - approached us.

'That's Kenny Dalglish, son,' my dad whispered. 'Right,' I blurted out. 'Who's he? 'My dad looked a tad embarrassed at my ignorance and nudged me quiet before greeting Kenny like an old friend he hadn't met in years. 'Hello Kenny. When are you going to get into this team?'

Kenny looked up shyly and replied, 'Nae chance!'

A Setirday Efternin

Paul Colvin

A poke o' chips an' Irn Bru, scoffed an' guzzled doon

How I used tae dae a' this, wi' only hauf a croon

Jumpin' oan a 64, the Auchenshuggle bus

Ma wid ayways worry an' make an awfy fuss.

A tanner fur a ticket an' that wis a return

Two bob left an' loaded, wi' money left tae burn

Ah'm nearly in the country, ah've jist passed through the toon

How ah used tae dae a' this wi' only hauf a croon.

Passin' by The Calton an' askin' who're the Tongs

Hauf a mile doon the road ah'd see the Celtic throngs

If ah wanted in the day, ah'd best be pretty swift

Cos ah've still tae ask: hey mister gaunny gie's a lift!

Seturday in Paradise queuin' at the gate

Ah'm gaun tae see the Celtic an' ah can hardly wait

Staunin' in the Sellick end cheerin' oan the 'Tic

Singin' a' the songs while Jinky done his tricks.

Hauf time came, ye ran doonsterrs, ah'd money left tae buy

A big hot cup o' Bovril and a greasy mutton pie

A healthy Glesga diet but it wis jist the ance a week

The Bovril wis aye roastin' an' you could hardly speak

55

The second hauf wis brulliant, we won the gemme three wan

Twelve years old, long troosers, ah'm near enough a man

It wisnae hard tae get there but comin' back's a joke

So ah guzzled wan mair Irn Bru an' kept mah chips hot in their poke!

They Gave Us James McGrory

Pat Marrinan

'Jimmy, it's time to get up,' whispered Harry McGrory in his soft Donegal accent. Sometimes he hated waking his son. The lad seemed happier in his dreams than the everyday poverty of Glasgow's tough Garngad district.

Jimmy's dark eyes were clotted with sleep, but he smiled at his Da and then, remembering today was the day of his brother John's funeral, his smile faded. 'What time are we due at St Roch's, Da?' he asked.

'An hour or so to go yet, son. Get dressed and have a good wash. Put on your school clothes. Yer Ma is making some breakfast in the scullery.'

Jimmy got up and glanced out the window of their tenement at 179 Millburn Street. It was quiet, the old buildings blackened by the smoke and soot of heavy industry, and the nearby gas works dilapidated and dirty grey. He dressed quietly, sat on his bed, closed his eyes and prayed for his brother John, lost to meningitis just a month after his first birthday.

'Jimmy, your breakfast is out, son,' called his mother from behind the curtain separating the kitchen from the big room, jolting him out of his prayers.

Jimmy opened his eyes, blessed himself and headed for the smell of toast wafting through the chilly flat.

His mother looked him over as he entered the kitchen. 'Yer looking smart, son, we'll get you some boots before winter.'

Jimmy glanced down at the threadbare school uniform and black sandshoes he wore every day. It was not in his nature to moan, especially since many of the other boys at St Roch's Primary school were worse off. Some even came to school barefoot in the better weather.

Da slipped out to the first floor landing hoping nobody would be in the communal cludgie, while Ma waited for Jimmy to finish his breakfast and wash his face in the kitchen sink. When it was time they made the short walk down the hill to St Roch's. Neighbours nodded solemnly as they passed.

'Sorry for your loss,' said Dan Murphy, shaking Harry McGrory gently by the hand, a wistful expression on his face.

Others neighbours stood on the pavements, heads bowed, in silence. A few blessed themselves. The funeral journey of the McGrory family was one many families in the Garngad took during those hard years after the First World War. Infant mortality in slum areas was a national disgrace and, as always, the poorest carried the heaviest burden.

Jimmy genuflected as he'd been taught when entering the nave of St. Roch's. The flimsy wood of the little coffin waiting for them by the altar carried a heavy burden. Tears welled in his eyes for little John but also for his parents. He glanced at his father knelt on the kneelers to his left, eyes closed, rosary beads in his hand.

A decent, hard-working dad who signed Jimmy's birth certificate with a cross because he couldn't write. A common labourer who sweated for more than 60 hours a week in the gas works and took all the overtime available to try and feed his family.

His ma, Kate McGrory, was worn out, old before her time, the wearying effects of poverty and child-bearing colouring her face, shaping her thin body as she sat in the pew next to his Da. Her faith in God helped carry her after losing John, which was also a test of her proud Irish heritage, but for the sake of the rest of her children she remained stoic and immensely proud of every single one of them.

He sat quietly in the rapidly filling Church and glanced at the image of Christ on the cross suspended high above the altar. 'Help me,' he whispered to his God. 'Help me to help them.'

Aged twelve Jimmy left primary school, not long after attending his mother's funeral. To help him deal with such a loss he lived and breathed football. The streets and cobbled back courts of the Garngad, uneven and rutted as they were, became his testing ground. Like many others around him football in those courts and streets provided an outlet for their energy and a temporary escape from the overcrowded homes, hunger and disease. Here they could imagine being stars of Maley's great Celtic team. A team they read about in the papers but few could afford to go and see. In these rough, open-ended street games McGrory toughened up and developed his skills. Sometimes the older, rougher kids lunged into tackles or tested his mettle by bad mouthing him. Jimmy always smiled and let his football do the talking. Games went on for hours and, when the last players drifted home, young Jimmy often borrowed the ball and played it off the tenement wall, practicing heading, control and shooting. Some nights he lay exhausted in his bed, mind whirling, thinking how to improve his physique and footballing ability.

One bright morning, as he left Mass, he was approached by the austere but much respected Canon Lawton. 'James, we're starting a football team in the area and I was wondering if you'd like to play for us?'

Young McGrory hesitated. He was desperate to play but didn't possess a decent pair of boots.

Canon Lawton went on, 'Of course, we'll supply strips and boots. We might even manage a pound or two a week if we get a decent crowd?'

Jimmy signed up for St Roch's Juniors that day.

For a boy of sixteen Junior football might have seemed intimidating but young McGrory excelled. He evaded the rash tackles with speed and athleticism, and his prowess at heading a ball had onlookers amazed. His physique responded to the regular training sessions and he grew into a powerful young man.

More importantly, in some ways, the £2 a week helped alleviate the McGrory family's poverty.

In 1922 McGrory scored in the final of the Scottish Junior Cup as St Roch's brought the trophy back to the Garngad for the first and only time. A coal lorry drove through the cheering crowds with the team, including young Jimmy, on the back.

Jimmy was happy being a good Junior player. Like all young players he'd wonder if he had what it took to play at senior level. In the darkness of his

59

room he'd lie awake and imagine pulling on the famous hoops of the team he supported all his life. He'd drift to sleep imagining the roar of the crowd as he slammed the ball into the net. But that was a distant dream. He knew thousands of boys like him dreamed of playing for Celtic. But none of them were Jimmy McGrory.

'Jimmy,' shouted his wee sister as he walked through the Garngad. 'Don't be giving all your wages away today eh?'

He smiled ruefully. 'I've only got a few bob on me. Will you stop worrying?'

She looked at him, a mothering smile on her face, 'Get the tram home then if it's raining.'

Jimmy walked quickly with his head down through the streets of depression-hit Glasgow. There would be no tram home after training, though. He was as easy a mark as he was a marksman-- every beggar and down-at- heel Glaswegian who asked him for a copper was met with a patient smile and couple of coins. By the time he reached Celtic Park McGrory hadn't a penny in his pocket. It was not an unusual occurrence for the club's new hotshot striker.

Even The Jungle Was Singing

Michael Maher

"Better than Lisbon!" That was what Jock Stein said and I knew just what he meant. He was talking about Celtic's League Cup victory over Rangers the previous night. It might have seemed odd to an outsider that a domestic win in the third, and least important, tournament in Scotland would elicit such a statement but the Celtic fans understood the big man's comments.

Before big Jock took over at Celtic Park it never occurred to me that Celtic might win the League. In the five years I'd been supporting Celtic the title was won by Rangers, Dundee and Kilmarnock, with Celtic never in the hunt. Then the world changed. Not only had we won the League for the last two seasons but a few months earlier I'd stood in the Estadio Nacional in Lisbon and watched Celtic win the European Cup. It was great to be Champions of Europe but it was still great to beat the Rangers. In those first five years of my Celtic life Celtic won only one of the ten Old Firm League encounters. Under big Jock I had the chance to even up the score.

So when the 1967/68 season started I was anxious that not only should we be seen as a genuine top European side but I wanted to maintain our dominance over the Ibrox men. We got the chance to meet early in the season as both Old Firm clubs were drawn in the same League Cup section along with Aberdeen and Dundee United. The North East clubs hadn't yet reached the status they would achieve in the 1980's but trips to Tannadice and Pittodrie were still dangerous. On the opening day Celtic scrambled a 1-0 win over United with a nineteenth minute Jimmy Johnstone goal. The Dons and Rangers drew at Pittodrie so Celtic were a point clear when they went to Ibrox the following midweek. That was still the case after the game. More than 94,000 saw Tommy Gemmell's penalty give Celtic a half-time lead. When Ronnie Simpson saved an Andy Penman penalty both points appeared bound for Celtic Park. But two minutes from time Penman, who had failed from 12 yards, equalised direct from a free kick 25 yards out. Both teams won their next two games so the stage was set for the big one. The return match was at Celtic Park on Wednesday 30th August. Celtic still had a point lead but if Rangers won they would leap-frog a point clear. Their last game was at home to United, while Celtic had a trip to Pittodrie.

As usual school lessons were hard to cope with at the start of the week of the big game. There were plenty of Celtic Supporters at St Patrick's High School in Coatbridge and the game was a main topic of conversation. It was, however, not the only big event to be decided that evening. The long-running TV series "The Fugitive" would be showing its final episode that night and the world would at last find out if Dr. Richard Kimble had indeed murdered his wife, or if it was the mysterious one-armed man. I hadn't been an avid follower of the series but would have watched the final episode except, of course, there was a much bigger decider taking place nearer home.

At last the day of the game arrived. I got home from school and got ready as quickly as possible. As a youngster it was a short tram or bus trip from Baillieston to Parkhead. In my early teens my family moved a bit further out to Bellshill but it was still a relatively easy journey with plenty of buses going into Glasgow from Bellshill Cross. Normally public transport took me to Celtic Park. However, for Old Firm games I felt safety in numbers was the best bet, so for this match I boarded the Bellshill & District CSC for the trip to Paradise. Soon we were parking in a rubble-strewn area beside the railway embankment that ran behind the Celtic End. I pushed myself through the crowd to catch up with school friends at our usual place – about halfway up the terracing behind the goals at the Celtic End. This was an important spot for us as we were part of the "Celtic Choir". Without the backing of the thousands of voices in the Celtic End the team would surely not perform as well. Contrary to what many people seem to think the "Jungle" was not the place for singing in those days. The Jungle inhabitants could be fierce in their partisan support but singing was not normally part of their scene.

You could never be really sure who started a song but it didn't take long to be taken up. Especially in a packed terracing where you'd be jostling and pushing to keep your position. And, of course, we had plenty to sing about. First-up came the chance to goad the Rangers fans at the other end-

"Champions of Europe, Champions of Europe…"

Then the tit- for- tat singing started in earnest as the sound from the opposite end of the ground drifted towards us-

"God save our gracious Queen, long live our noble queen....."

"Soldiers are we, whose lives are pledged to Ireland... "

The crowd was building up towards the 75,000 mark and the chanting became louder and more passionate.

"It is old and it is beautiful and its colours they are fine ...." "It was on a dreary New Year's Eve as the shades of night came down....." "With heart and hand and sword and shield we'll guard old Derry's Walls..' "We're off to Dublin in the green, in the green...."

We hadn't reached kick-off but already we'd put in a good shift supporting the Bhoys. It was a mild autumn night and I sweated up against other bodies and felt the sense of anticipation pass through us The teams came out to a great roar and soon the game was underway.

After eight minutes a through ball from Rangers midfield found Willie Henderson all on his own. Very much on his own. Must be offside I thought as he put the ball in the Celtic net. And then that moment-- unique to Old Firm games. Complete silence at the Celtic End. And then you hear it. That rumbling, almost muffled, noise from the other end as you realise Rangers have indeed scored. It was a perfect example of sound travelling slower than light. Those seconds seemed to last for several minutes before we came out of our collective trance.

Voices beside me heckled: "Offside! He was a mile offside".

The Celtic players appealed to the referee, Tiny Wharton, and the linesman but the goal stood. Anger grew all around me.

"Ya big Orange Bastard!"

"Always the same – we get nothing from these people."

Celtic pushed for the equaliser and Bobby Lennox got the ball in the net. Cheers were short lived. This time, of course, the offside flag did go up. Words and oaths were spat out with venom.

"What did ah tell ye? – Cheatin' Masonic bastards."

"C'mon Celtic get right intae these people."

Half- time and Rangers were still in the lead.

Despite our constant encouragement we headed into the last fifteen minutes 0-1 down. Celtic still pressed but Rangers defended the goal at the Rangers End like their lives depended on it.

Suddenly, there was a breakaway. Once again Willie Henderson raced through on the Celtic goal. This time there was no doubt he was onside. John Clark tried to catch him. Ronnie Simpson started to come off his line. Just as the Ibrox winger was about to shoot Luggy tackled him from behind, bringing him down in the box. No protests in the Celtic End. It was a stonewaller. John Clark could have been sent off but it seemed a penalty was punishment enough. If Rangers scored they'd go two up and top of the section. Deflation in the Celtic End.

I had been going to games with Peter Dickson for years, and usually he was the eternal optimist, but after watching us press for almost the entire game without scoring and getting nothing off the officials he shrugged, "It's not our night. I'm heading home."

I was never one for leaving early so I shouted to persuade him to wait a bit longer. Just as he turned round Kaj Johansen stepped up to take the kick. He shot and .... hit the bar! The ball bounced down from the bar and back towards the Dane. Instinctively, he reached forward to header it.

I wasn't sure of the referee's impartiality so along with many others I yelled – "He cannae dae that!"

Johansen realised this, too, and tried to duck, but was too late. He touched the ball again before any other player. Even a biased referee couldn't ignore such a blatant infringement.

Now the Celtic End was literally jumping again.

I got a surprise when I bounced against my uncle James. He told me he'd left when Rangers were awarded the penalty. On hearing the cheers from the Celtic fans he ran back into the ground. As he started climbing the steps leading into the middle of the Celtic End he looked above and could see the concrete terracing shaking. He hesitated for a few seconds before rushing back in for the last twelve minutes.

And what a twelve minutes. We were in full voice again.

"For it's a grand old team to play for" as Celtic attacked down the left

"and it's a grand old team to see" – Corner for Celtic

"and if you know the history..." GOAL-!! Willie Wallace bundled the cross from the corner over the line. Three-quarters of the ground were ecstatic.

We might not have needed divine help but some request to a higher power never went amiss. "Hail Glorious St Patrick, dear Saint of Our Isle," started in the Celtic end. Like the "Celtic Song" this one was being picked up by the Jungle

"On Erin's green valleys, on Erin's green valleys , On--.." GOAL! Bobby Murdoch slammed a shot into the Rangers net. We were in the lead with seven minutes to the final whistle and the body language of the players told us there was only one winner.

"Go home ya Huns, Go home ya Huns.. " The away terracing started to empty. In the eighty-ninth minute Bobby Lennox put the green and white icing on all our cakes with a third.

The final whistle soon followed. What a victory. We had to be good to beat Inter Milan but to beat Rangers we had to beat more than eleven men and we did. We levitated out into Janefield Street. I bumped into my cousin Johnny. He had been watching from his usual stance in the Jungle. There was a broad smile on his face. He rasped at me, his voice hoarse: "What a game- Even the Jungle was singing!" Soon I was back on the bus listening to everyone talking at once about the game. Feelings of elation from such a victory gave our body and mind a glow that no earthly drug could provide.

When we got to Bellshill Cross I got off quickly -- I wanted to get home to see the highlights on Sportscene.

"Wait a minute," said Mick Cassidy. "Wait till the others are ready, just in case there are a few angry bears out there. Safety in numbers."

There was, however, no bother as a group of us headed down the North Road.

Chic Doherty lived close-by and walked with me to my door. His first Celtic game was a 6-2 win over Rangers in the 1930's. "They were the People, Michael" he said. "Not anymore!"

I got in just in time to watch the TV highlights and could tell immediately by my father's beaming face that he already knew the score. "What a game Dad- what a night, we did it!"

"Aye," he said. "Celtic did it and Richard Kimble didn't!"

Jimmy Johnstone

Paul Colvin

He joined Celtic, aged thirteen years, a ballboy at the game

The youth team knocked upon his door, his skill had gained him fame

The bhoy from Viewpark Uddingston, would stake an early claim

To become the greatest ever Celt, the world has ever seen.

A Glasgow bhoy, a Celtic man, he always knew he'd play

In front of sixty thousand fans in Paradise one day

He played the game to entertain, enthralling all the crowd

And in return, the fans would sing, his praises loud and proud.

Our winger showed his trickery, his guile and his strength

His attitude, his balance, poise, displayed at every length

He'd jink around the same man twice, that's how he got his name

He'd twist and turn 'til they were dazed, then take them on again.

Diminutive in stature, a Colossus on the field

He stood a measly five feet four but this man would never yield

His fiery, ginger, curly hair and mesmerising moves

Inspired at an early age to play the game he loves.

His dazzling skills and flight of feet were wondrous to see

Defenders terrified of him would want to turn and flee

They knew they'd never catch him, so kicked him as before,

A Foul! He'd just take the ball and go back in for more!

His football became legendary, across the globe did span

The attitude he always showed, to please the paying fan

By skipping past the midfield men and flying down the wing

From there he'd beat them yet again, and his cross, a goal would bring.

Jinky relished every game and wore his shirt with pride

Bobbing, weaving in and out, he'd star in any side

A master craftsman of his art, always brave and bold

A solo genius, never rich, was worth his weight in gold.

Diseased with Motor Neurone, he sadly passed away

The legacy he left to us, the wonders of his play.

Lord Of The Wing, we thank you, you made that No 7

All your own and wear it still, in your Paradise in Heaven.

Sun Shines On East End

Lorenzo Wordsmith

Today the sun shines brightly on East End walk, it signals vitality, it signals life.

Tested travellers gaze in memory to days of old, they amaze at, Oh, how landscape changes, the welcome view smiles generously, so pleasing to the eye.

Fresh young faces take in their generation, noticing only immediate difference as mere yearly changes with growing pains in stages, so engaged to end in sheer delight.

Changes indeed as subtle as strip design a hoop, still fully aware of the rugged sign of previous defiance. Shown and thrown from proudest breast from such magnificence in ageing crest, that rock on which was built all safe and sound foundation.

No sight of an older cash strapped plight, no sign of relent in dogged fight, no laden wagon of deposit ore, the parade of history steeped deep to core, in days of progress now at the fore, to delight this newest age.

In God's green land the turning page flicks comfortably through rivers of strong support, now fully immersed in another chapter, the next stage.

For this is no coincidence, there is no mystery, it is written so, in one's own book of Celtic legend, it breathes easily inside.

Where there was that new beginning, there shall be no end.

For within this new horizon, within this new vista, the Celtic vision beats stronger and still so true, the same as it ever was.

Today the sun shines brightly like all our yesterdays, as will our tomorrows, on the East End walk.

The Davie Moyes Partnership

Jack O'Donnell

Yellow acrylic curtains and Venetian blinds form a clinking wind-blown shutter keeping out the wintery dregs of submarine daylight. The bedroom light clicks. Mum hauls the handlebars of my shoulder and shakes till my neck and head lollop into a semblance of something human.

'There's a letter for you.' Mum's sing-song voice has come to torture me.

My arms wave about like antennas and the white quivering mass of my body burrows deeper into the mattress shell, snuffling and sucking the last vestiges of heat from the three layers of blankets swamping my bed. I groan the Esperanto of sleep language, yawn, and shake off that weighty hand. I figure the heavy responsibility of school is waiting to happen day after day and would be lighter without my presence.

'Hurry up. It's time to get up.' Mum targets the carapace of bedclothes hitched around my shoulders and neck, but I've a glacial grip of them. 'You've got a letter,' she reminds me.

Cloth-eared, the slip and slide of slippered feet move away following the worn sluggard trail on the diamond patterned linoleum around the wooden footboard of my bed. My gummy eyes squint open. Mum leans over my wee brother, Bod, and pats his helmet hair.

'Bryan!' A halo of exhalation marks Mum's neck-nuzzling. She hovers over him, breathing him in, whispering, in a nursery-rhyme voice, 'time to get up'.

Bod's eyes open. He falls sideways, feet first, out of bed and stumbles along like a bumble-bee drifting between our beds. Mum's hand is on the baby-blue stripes of his pyjama top, guiding him down the hall and towards the toilet.

I turn over in disgust, but keeping my eyes shut now would be like cheating. I've a stiffy that needs careful handling. I can't work out if it's because I desperately need to pee, which I do, or just have a hard-on because I've a hard-on. Either way I need into the toilet fast. I knuckle against the hallway wall and walk crab ways, my pecker in my Y-fronts pointing in the right direction.

Mum's back at her usual slot at the sink in the kitchen. She's put a plate of Cornflakes on the kitchen table for me. Scooping them up and over my wee brother's head I'm careful not to slop milk as I carry them through to the warmth of the living room. Perched on the seat near the window, kitchen door pulled partially shut, spooning breakfast into my gob, I try to avoid listening to The Hairy Cornflake, Diddy Dave Lee Travis, on the radio and the incessant drone of Mull of Kintyre that is played after every second record and lasts longer than talk of the Second World War. I tip the plate up to drink down gooey sugar and the last of the Cornflakes. Finished, I nick out into the hall and head back into the Siberia of my room. I fling stuff into my Adidas holdall for PE later and add a Math book and unlined jotter before circling back into the living room. I peer at the clock at the centre of the mantelpiece flanked by a red statue of a bearded Jesus and a blue statue of The Virgin Mary on the other, but with a squinty head, because it's been chalked and knocked off a few times, but nobody in our family admits to having dunted it. The Holy Mother doesn't seem to mind such common-place miracles of beheading. She's used to an ocean of suffering. Big Ben is ten minutes fast to encourage us to be early, but sometimes it's fifteen, or has even been known to be twenty, which is too much, warps time, and made us late, which I don't mind either.

A business envelope slants from under one of the peeling mock-gold clock legs. I don't often get letters, not official ones with a First-class stamp. I rustle the paper against my ear and sniff at the sealed edges and there's a weighty smell like a new anorak. My name's typed directly onto the envelope and I hold the corners of the brown sleeve in each hand, out in front of me, as if it's ticking to see how it looks from far away. Fag smoke drifts through from the kitchen. I reel my neck sideways to check Mum's still next door before running my index finger along the glued edge. I pick out the white card with a thick green band with a thinner gold lying on top, the Shamrock crest and legend Celtic Boys' Club centred. I tear open the letter and read it so many times I could mimic the signature at the bottom of the page and the slanted letters in blue biro p.p. something or other.

I'd prayed and prayed and prayed I'd play for Celtic. I thanked God and the Devil and didn't care which. I wonder whether the scout was at the game against St. Kessog's on their tight gravel park in Balloch-- I'd put their big centre-forward on his arse twice. Mr. Callan, the Guild manager, said I'd been our best player, even though we got beaten by a couple of goals. The Catholic-atheistic part of me argued that God hadn't really been involved and it was one of my uncle's pals that had sent me the club's invite, as he'd drunkenly promised to do, sight unseen, but with a picture of The Sacred Heart looking down and bleeding from the living room wall, I didn't want to dwell overlong on such heresies.

Mum steps through to the living room with a scrunched dish towel, wiping at her hands and an Embassy Mild tight in her lips. Without her specs she makes a face at the clock and takes a quick drag before speaking. 'Shouldn't you be away?'

I remain transfixed, the letter in my hand, but she catches the excitement in my eyes.

'What? What?' she asks.

'Celtic under-fifteen's have told me to come and play with them.' Grinning, my head dropping modestly, as I correct myself, waving the letter at her, 'well, train with them'.

'That's great.'

Mum draws me into her arms. The familiar balm of stale fags and sweat shrouds me. I let her give me a quick cuddle, even though I'm far too old for that kind of malarkey. I've a decko at the time over her shoulder. If I hurry I'll just get, or just miss, the twenty-to-nine bus for school. I place the envelope and letter back on the mantelpiece under Big Ben's luminous clock face, but slip the card in the back pocket of my tan cords as a reminder.

Three of the guys in my school team, St Andrew's, already play for Celtic Boys' Club under-fifteens and they come from the same area of Whitecrook. Curly- haired Benny Hagen is a bit of a punk, but he doesn't need to rip or pin his everyday clothes much to be one. He pogoes with real style at St Stephen's Guild discos to the sound of The Sex Pistols, 'Pretty Vacant'. At football he's all left foot, but balanced on the curve of an angel's wings and can go one way or the other. He's ballsy and tricky as Satan and I know if anyone can become a professional footballer, it'll be Benny.

John McKeever is called Bonny, a legacy, I suppose, from when he was a baby. He's still a wee guy, with shoulder-length hair, but Bonny keeps himself very fit, with weights and running and has a football brain. He always knows where he is on a football park and a size-five Mitre is a friend.

Norrie McGlinchy is sleek as a black-haired otter, but with pneumatic lips. He'd lost a couple of toes, when his foot got caught in the school gate when he was younger, but with a ball is relatively two-footed. He's a winger that whips balls into the box and scores goals.

I've a bit of everything the Whitecrook lads have. I've curly hair, can pogo with the worst of them, I'm stocky as Bonnie and if my left foot was removed nobody would notice when I play football.

I don't bug them, but incessantly finger the card in my pocket throughout the day. I'm determined to make a go of my God-given opportunity, give it everything I have to play for my beloved Celtic, be utterly dedicated, but can't remember if training at Barrowfield on a Thursday night is the same night Starsky and Hutch is on telly.

Lugging a school bag and try-out kit to school is a hassle I can do without. My Adidas Samba are banana curled at the toe and stink, but only if you put your nose near the mouth of the plastic bag. I diddle-dawdle all day for the bell to go at four o'clock and when it does I'm not ready. The Perspex bus shelter outside the school keeps the rain at bay, but not the wind, and I clomp three steps backwards and forwards to keep fit and to give myself something to do. Spirals pointing heavenward, Our Holy Redeemer's across the road glooms down at me as a reminder, of what, I'm not quite sure. I've an extra 60p to get me up and back, which I jingle-jangle in my bomber-jacket pocket, worried I don't have enough money. McClaren's, on the ground floor of the tenement beside the chapel, shop lights are on and it's still open. I think about ditching training and just going home with some sweets and a few ice- poles. But my Da, who walks everywhere, told me the Auchenshuggle would take me straight there. He'd have strolled the seven or eight miles to Barrowfield. That would have been his training. Da's a bit like a bomber pilot when giving directions, a bus going straight there to him meant being within three or four miles of the target. It's the East End of Glasgow and I know from going to the Celtic games that a stranger's face can mean trouble. I'm relieved and disappointed when the 64 bus rattles past Simeone's chip shop, where we sometimes got our lunchtime rolls, picks up speed passing my school, St Andrew's, and the Auchenshuggle splashes up alongside the bus stop and jerks to a juddering stop, the engine spilling out a fug of diesel fumes. The driver turns his head to look at me to see if I'm a passenger or a chancer.

Most of the downstairs seats are taken. I scuttle upstairs to the smokers and sit in the seat directly above the driver with a panoramic view. An old woman, about thirty-five, with a long black leather coat tight around her thin shoulders sits smoking on the double seat opposite mine. She glances up at me then stares out the side window. Three or four shopping bags are positioned as perishable barriers on the seat beside her. The conductress climbs up the stairs behind me. Her ginger hair is in flight, sticking out of her head sideways, a cantilever bridge frozen in place by hairspray, but smiles as she asks for the fare and checks my ticket. With the stop- start roll of the bus in the traffic at Yoker, her hand rests on my shoulder and she swears she'll tell me when we get to Barrowfield. It's a straight road from then on, but I clutch the metal grip bar waiting for sudden swerves and turns. Gloaming twilight is crowned by the neon light of city-centre stores. The bus picks up speed again. Buildings become more spaced out and derelict and my neck's an elastic band twisting backwards and forwards. I eventually pluck up the courage to ask the conductress if we're there yet. Her answer's as unwavering as her hair-- four more stops and that's us at London Road.

A man in dark oil-stained overalls, minging of booze, gets off at the same stop as me and I ask him where Barrowfield is. Dead-eyed, he looks me over for a few seconds. I clutch at my plastic bag and stick my pigeon-chest out that extra inch.

'Papes over there,' he said.

Da was right, even I couldn't really miss it. There are lots of guys my age hanging about. I spot Benny Hagen's curly head and that's me sorted.

The changing rooms are a pre-fabricated concrete shell with benches and showers. Benny nods me towards the under-fifteen's manager, a puggish wee guy called Bobby Brown. The other trainees know each other and joke around as they get changed. Bobby takes me aside. As he reads his index finger quickly runs down the letter I received. I show him the business card. He leaves me standing and has a confab with an older man wearing moulded football boots. He's taller, with a sandbox body poured into a green tracksuit and a squarish head, covered by short Brillo-pad hair.

Training outside is just the usual stuff of running fast and slow in circles round the football pitch, but because it's Celtic Boys' Club it's dressed up with dancing quick-step between cones and ball work. The coaches lay the ball off right of left and we file into two groups at opposite ends of the park. We have a laugh and shoot into the nets with the goalie trying to save it. The banter of the other boys tell me that on the other gravel park Charlie Nicholas is top goal scorer of the under-sixteen's, on an S-form, and expected to shine. I sneak a look at him. His finishing is a tad better than mine.

Two spotlights bolted on the side of the pre-fab throw sixpence worth of lights onto the side-lines and it's spot the ball. Bobby hurriedly picks two teams for the bounce game. Davy (Shirley Temple) Moyes whose hair falls in natural red ringlets has protruding discus-shaped eyes and plays centre-half for the club. That's the position I told Bobby I played. Davy and I start as a loose partnership in defence, perhaps too loose. Norrie McGlinchy is in my team, the other Whitecrookonians from my school are in opposition to us. As the ball scoots about I notice from shouts and whistles a certain amount of deference is given by our manager to Shirley the under- fifteen's captain. The coach quickly moves me into midfield playing beside a tidy player called Buttons. I'm all humility. I listen to everything the coach bellows at me. I want to learn. I will learn, but I'm moved right-wing and there's nothing I can be taught because the ball continually shuttles up the left-wing to Norrie. My team troop off defeated and clatter into the changing rooms, where the under-sixteen's team are already getting showered.

Panting players, who've helped take the cones in, charge past and I join them. When we get showered there's no hot water left. Before we leave the changing room Bobby gathers us in a loose clique around him, with some of the boys standing on seats, looking over the metal grills. He tells us to meet here Saturday and who the opposition are. He reminds us it's a Scottish cup tie and we're the holders and have won it the last four out of five years. His parting shot is about wearing the club blazer, shirts and ties. Most of the trainees already have official green Celtic Boys' Club holdall-bags. I slink behind the Whitecrook boys with my Adidas and plastic bags to the bus stop and we all get the same bus home.

On Saturday I can't sleep and I'm up earlier than Mum. The morning drags. I hate wearing a shirt and tie. It takes me an hour to get to Barrowfield by bus. A few of the players I've met are kicking a ball around. I join them dirtying-up my shiny shoes which makes me feel better. The Whitecrook contingent comes last of all. They're easy about being late. My football boots are in my bag, polished and shiner than Guinness. I've a towel but don't bother with shin-pads. In the dressing room we sprawl out along the wooden benches. The hush as Bobby comes in with the team sheets is familiar as the caustic rub of Ralgex. He starts shouting out names and numbers. Players are getting changed even before their name is read out. When he gets to my lucky number four I hold my breath, but it's Bonnie, positioned sweeper, behind Shirley, number five. I hope, against disbelief, I'll be starting in midfield, but when he gets to eight, nine, ten, eleven- Benny and Norrie are in the team- I know I'll be a sub. He gets to number twelve and thirteen. Football studs castanet against the stone floor and there's a buzz of players getting changed. I shuffle sideways. Bobby sits at the end of one of the benches near the door, leaning in, talking quietly to one of the other coaches. I nod as I pass him and his eyebrows lift like a cheap rug as he looks up at me and I know, I just know—sometimes a manager finds it difficult to leave you out of his team and sometimes he doesn't know who you are.

Faith

Andy McCrimmon

I never had faith

Only in you

Never given the good book its due

Until I saw you,

Saw you sit with quiet cheer

While all around sit in fear

You have the good Lord's ear

I never had faith

Until I saw you

While all around fall to pieces

These children, all made from pieces

Of you

I never had faith

Only in you

I pray I am wrong

When body has gone,

Soul will go on,

In the taste of a celebratory mint

Or in a crossword hint

Or in the boy with the blue eyed glint

I never much cared for chapel

Not the snake and the apple

Until I saw you

Saw you flick through the Celtic View

Euro Final 1970

Eric Belton

Early on the morning of the final we made our way to Cochrane Street, near George Square in Glasgow, to join a coach party for the onward journey to Prestwick Airport. We were on our way to Milan.

I'd travelled by aeroplane on three previous occasions - to Dublin, Brussels and Barcelona, - but this was the first to watch Celtic. And with it being a European Cup Final I was so excited I wasn't sure I needed a plane to fly.

Once settled into the flight it became clear that The Phil Cole Celtic Supporters Club of Coatbridge had booked in bulk for this Celtic invasion of Milan. Club members kindly distributed green and white hats to us all, whether members or not, and this kindness would be further illustrated later in the flight.

The journey was fairly uneventful. Celtic songs were sung with gusto. Predictably, the air hostesses, as they tried to demonstrate the intricacies of the life jacket, were given a hard time by the excited, or I should say, nervous passengers. Many of them, flying for the first time, hadn't considered the prospect of requiring a life-jacket, but it added to the festive atmosphere.

It was announced that the plane was descending towards Malpensa Airport, which should have been a hint to be seated. However, I noticed a club member, oblivious to such rules, making his way from front to back, speaking to the folk on either side. When he came in line I asked him what was happening.

He responded, quite officiously, well he was the treasurer after all, "I'm passing the hat round for the driver!"

Now we were no jet setters, but we had a notion as to what the "driver's" salary was likely to be. In time honoured fashion, however, we added our contribution to the already sagging, coin-filled bunnet.

A short time later, the pilot announced, in a rather posh accent, that it was not policy to accept gratuities. Once the definition of gratuity became better understood by some of the more inebriated, rumblings of discontent grew louder, only for the pilot to quickly see sense and thank the supporters for their kindness, wishing Celtic success in the final.

The rest, as they say, is history.

Lisbon Lions Day

William McNeill

This day is called – the feast of Lisbon Lions Day:

He that plays on this day, and comes safe home,

Will stand a tip-toe when this day is named,

And smile at the name of Jock Stein.

He that outlives this day, and sees old age,

Will yearly on this vigil feast his friends,

And say, "Today is Lisbon Lions Day."

Then he will hold out his hand, and show his medal,

And say, "This I won on Lisbon Lions Day."

Old men forget: yet all shall be forgot,

But he'll remember, with advantages,

What feats we did that day.

Then shall their names,

Familiar in his mouth as household words,

Simpson, Craig, Gemmell, Murdoch, and McNeill,

Clark, Johnstone and Wallace,

Chalmers, Auld and Lennox,

Be in their cups freshly remembered.

This story shall the good man teach his son;

And Lisbon Lions Day shall ne'er go by

From this day to the ending of the world,

But in it we shall be remembered, -

We few, we happy few, we band of brothers.

For he who shares Lisbon Lion Day with me,

Shall be my brother, be he ne'er so vile,

This day shall gentle his condition:

And those people in Edmiston Drive,

Shall think themselves cursed, they were not here,

And hold their manhoods cheap, while any speaks,

That played with us upon Lisbon Lions Day.

The Red-Haired Man

David Scott

I got a phone call last night from my mate Eddie who was totally freaked out about something that happened at the game. I kinda wish he hadn't as it's a bit creepy, but in a really nice way. I know, that sounds weird. To put you in the picture he's a very down to earth guy and that's what makes it worse. He takes his two grandkids to the games and gives them shots each. It's a really long story so I asked him to send me an email about what happened. I have edited it a little to correct a few bits of spelling and tried to make it fit the page better. I think it's worth sharing.

From: Eddie Caird < xxxxxxxx@yahoo.co.uk This email address is being protected from spambots. You need JavaScript enabled to view it.

> To: David Kennedy < David@Sxxxxxxxxx.com This email address is being protected from spambots. You need JavaScript enabled to view it.

> Reply-To: Keith McDowall < xxxxxxx@yahoo.co.uk This email address is being protected from spambots. You need JavaScript enabled to view it.

> Subject: Re: ghost Date: Thu, 29 Dec 2011 16:00:24 +0000 (GMT) X-Mailer: YahooMailWebService/0.8.115.331698

Hi Davy,

Here's that email you asked me to send. I am shite at writing things down and it might not come across very well but I will do my best. Please edit out anything you think isn't right. I will try to relay some of the bits of conversation I had with the wee yin but it might look crap. You know where I sit. Last night there was a couple of seats next to me at the aisle empty as the two Irish bhoys hadn't made it over. They weren't empty all night as a few lads had sat down and then went away again. I think there was a few sneaked in so there was a bit of coming and going. I know you asked me if you could post this online so for people that don't know me I'll fill in a few bits. I never slept a wink last night and I can't stop thinking about what happened. You can ask the wee yin yourself when you see her. Honest to God I near shit masel. You can delete that bit.

Okay here's the picture for the guys online that don't know me. I am 52 yo and I have two season books in the Jock Stein. I take my two grandkids on alternate games and this last night at the Rangers game I took my Grand Daughter Abbey. I wouldn't normally take a nine year old to a Rangers game but we had a reserved disabled parking space right at the door and I was going to leave early because she was there.

So what happened? I am still getting shivers.

We were doing all the usual stuff and singing and dancing and I was getting right into it. There were piles of really bad language but well a young girl has to learn sometimes. We were having great fun and, as you know, the atmosphere was brilliant. There was an empty seat to our left and sometimes two empty seats at the aisle to our right. The first two seats opposite the aisle were Kenny and Andy's seats. Kenny also has grandkids and always brings a wee Celtic picture or a badge for Abbey or Katie and they love him to bits. Abbey always shouts across to them and they wind her up, so it's not unusual to see her turned round and talking across the aisle.

I was a bit carried away with the game and didn't pay Abbey quite as much attention as usual, but she was always talking across the aisle to auld Andy and she was having a ball. Everything was normal for an Old Firm game. At half time I asked her what Andy had been saying. She said it was too loud and she couldn't hear; she just chatted to the nice man that sat beside her. "The wee guy with the daft hat?" I said.

"No Granda, the nice man with the red hair."

Oh Ok. Fair enough. I thought nothing more of it and we danced and sang and cheered. We left with 15 minutes to go. I never leave early but it was a Rangers game and I wanted to get Abbey safely home. On the way out she started to laugh and I saw her putting something inside her coat. I assumed it was her match programme. We got back to the car and got away from Paradise super quick. We were happy and listened to the end of the game on the radio and, as we got to the start of Springburn Road, the game ended with us jumping about like a pair of dafties. Well jumping about as much as you could inside a Nissan Sunny.

I'll try to recap the conversation in the car as best I can. Ask Abbey yourself at the weekend. I swear on the Holy Bible this was exactly as it went:

"What bit did you like the best?"

Abbey: "The Goal. It was magic. It hurt my ears."

"Did auld Andy give you a badge?"

Abbey: "Naw. I couldn't speak to him, it was too loud."

"I saw you talking to him."

Abbey. "Naw. I was talking to the man."

"What man?".

Abbey: "The nice man with the red hair. I liked him."

"Ah, I missed him. He must have moved away quick."

Abbey (laughing): "Daftie! He was there the whole game. You need to go to Specsavers."

Okayyyyyy, I thought, I'm not that old. She's winding me up. But I don't like strange men talking to her, and when people do chat to her I always listen. There's no way, even in the heat of a Rangers' game, I would have missed anyone talking to her.

"So what was this man saying?" I asked.

Abbey: "He was just telling me about how the game was going and that the game was good."

"Anything else?"

Abbey: "He said he used to wear the Celtic shirt and that he had friends still here."

"Did he tell you his name?"

Abbey: "Naw. I asked him, but he just smiled. He said you might know him though."

"He what? How the...? Did he say anything other than football stuff?"

Abbey: "Naw Granda. Just football!. Don't worry, he was awfy nice."

I was a bit freaky. I'd no recollection of this guy. I did see her talking to someone, but the seat was empty. I was also getting a bit angry- at myself- because, as you well know, I am really protective of her. We all are. But there's no way someone could have been at the game for seventy minutes talking to her and me not spotting him.

At this point I remembered that on our way out of the ground she'd put something in the inside jacket pocket. I was praying that it wasn't a phone number, or email address, or worse. In truth all sorts of shite went through my head and I was thinking stuff that I shouldn't be thinking.

"Did he give you anything?" I tried to coax it out of her without giving too much away about what I was thinking, but she was a step ahead of me.

Abbey: "Yep, but Granda he wasn't a perv!"

I nearly choked. "What did he give you?"

Abbey: "It's in my jacket, in the boot. It's ok Granda, it's cool and I was going to give it to you for your birthday-on Saturday."

"Sweetheart, I know you're a big girl, but if a strange person gives you something I really should know what it is."

Abbey: "Okay, I'll give it to you now if you like."

My temperature was rising, partly because I'd spoiled my birthday surprise and partly because I was being over protective and treating her as if she was even younger than she was. I hated doing that because she really is a smart wee cookie. Anyway, I drove into MacDonald's, in Springburn Road, ordered a drive thru and then sat in the car park. Abbey was full of nonsense, but I tried to keep my worries out of my voice.

"Abbs, go get the thing the man gave you will you, don't think I'm being an old fart."

Abbey: "Sure, you'll really like it. The man says it's a special thing and it's a won of..."

"...what's a won of?"

Abbey: "Dunno." She laughed as she said it, making me believe her.

Even now I can't stop thinking about. She went and brought out the thing the man had given her. It was beautiful. But I promised Abbey I wouldn't tell a living soul what it was, so I hope you understand I can't let her down.

Davy, let me say this. There's no way on earth that it could have been bought on the internet, or in a shop. It's the real deal. Abbey has slept with it beside her bed all night. It's the real thing. I knew instantly who it belonged to. I shit masel. My fingers shook. I knew the man. But I reasoned that it was maybe a relative. Did he have a brother? I asked myself.

Just before I dropped Abbey off I asked her, "Abbs are you sure the man never said his name?"

Abbey: "Nope. He told me he was a Gaulton Boy."

"Gaulton? Never heard of it, was it Galston?"

Abbey: "Em, don't think so."

"He didn't say anything else that would give you a clue to who he was?"

Abbey: "Oh yes, he said people called him a funny name."

"Can you remember what it was?"

Abbey didn't take it seriously and started laughing. "Aye that's easy, he said his name was 'Mr twists and turns'."

Davie, I swear on my grandkids' lives that's what she said. You can ask her. I'm a greetin' wreck. That thing he gave her could only have been his, or been bought by someone from him.

Later, Abbs was staying with us and she went to her bed early. I told her she could watch Shrek on the telly in the bedroom. That was when I phoned you. I haven't a clue what to do now. If anything, Abbey is incredibly happy and she's kept the thing beside her all night, every night and treasures it. What I didn't tell you last night though was sitting in the living room something jumped into my head and because Abbs was still watching the film I went into her room and asked her.

"Abbey, where did the man say he was from?"

"Gaulton Granda."

"Abbey, was it Calton?"

"Yayyyyyyyyy Granda that was it. Calton."

The Jungle Bhoys

Paul Colvin

Flat caps, soft hats, trilbies even tammies

Shuffling in their thousands and none feared any rammies.

Kids with men, and women too, they took their pride of place,

These Celtic spirits highly charged and most were off their face!

Pish ran down the concrete steps and sometimes down your legs

In your pocket, anywhere, they'd just shake off the dregs

You'd turn to see who done it, then quickly look away

Battered faces, scars, the lot, it just was not your day!

It's nearly time for kick-off and the stench near made you sick

The Jungle was now jumping as they welcomed on the 'Tic

The cheapest wines flowed down their necks, they were always willing

To drink their Lannie or El D, swilling for a shilling!

They suffered it for Celtic's sake, they said it helped them roar

And God, I didn't believe them, until the Celtic scored

You couldn't see or hear a thing above the Jungle's noise

Chaos ruled and polis ran to flee the Jungle Bhoys!

Hot pies tossed into the pish, gave off jets of steam

The smell was bloody awful, still they suffered for their team

But the atmosphere was something else, though most of them won't know

How they managed to get home or who played in Celtic's show!

They were having their own show, the rest just sang along

But Parkhead came to life for us when the Jungle was on song

Bring it back for just one day and let the young ones see the light,

So they can reminisce like me of wondrous Celtic nights.

Yes they've gone and dwindling crowds, may seem that we have lost

But inside you is where you'll find, that mighty Jungle's ghost

Love Street in the Rain

Kevin McCallum

I wake on an armchair, head banging like a Lambeg Drum and neck feeling like it's been gripped all night by Mick McManus. I'm in a council house not too far from home judging by the layout. But nothing else is familiar other than the Westclox on the wall above the mantelpiece. It's the same as my mum's and it's telling me to forget any wet dreams of a hot shower. I've fifteen minutes to get my arse to work. I tiptoe into the kitchen, trying not to wake the two bodies on the couch and run the cold water tap over the plastic basin full of mugs, plates and scummy water. My mouth fits around the tap and I drink half my body weight in water, then splash the other half on my face. A quick spike of my hair and I slip out the back door as if I'd stole the last bog roll.

The Carman Hills on the horizon confirm I'm somewhere up Bonhill. If I jog at a steady pace I'll make it to work in ten minutes and straighten myself up a bit in the process.

Nothing clears my head like an early morning run. Doesn't matter how heavy the night before -- blood gets pumping, adrenalin takes over and the competitive edge kicks in, even when just racing myself.

No sooner have I upped the pace and one of my slip-on sannies flies off my foot and on to the road, reminding me why they only cost £2. Picking the shoe up I have a flashback to arguing with my girlfriend last night. No doubt I've said something I shouldn't, like always. Probably something to do with the football, or her mates, like always. Fuck it, no doubt she'll be up to nip my nut tonight about it, like always

I curl my toes to try and keep my feet in my sannies as I pound the pavement to the same beat as the thumping in my head. Then it hits me. Jesus Christ! Never mind last night. Doesn't matter what happened last night, or the night before that. Personal crises have no bearing on today.

I slow down at the bottom of Bank Street, partly to think about the potential gravity of the day and partly because I'm fucked. My legs are willing, but my heart's palpitating more than usual. Whether that's from running or the thought of the game I'm not quite sure.

Hearts are still overwhelming favourites, though, and will have something to say about us winning the league. If it was a three-legged race they've already got two feet standing on the finishing line. All they have to do is stumble over it, which, going by the unbeaten run they're on, doesn't look likely. But I'm a bit daft that way. I've got the Celtic faith. Hearts luck can't last forever. They're not even the third best team in the country. Aberdeen and Dundee United are better. Dundee can beat them today. In fact, Dundee can pump them today. Mind you, Dundee are shite. I might have faith, but I'm not that kind of daft.

I start walking up the hill towards the shopping centre, sweat running down my face as if I've played the full ninety minutes. I've got things to think about. Davie Hay's also got things to think about. We need to do our bit at Love Street. It won't be easy but, if we play like we know we can, winning four goals to nothing is possible. It's more than possible. It's probable. What am I talking about? Why the fuck am I going to this stupid job? There'll be other jobs. I should be heading to Love Street. The jingle of loose coins in my pocket gives me an idea and I head to the phone box in Mitchell Way. Thing better be working.

I've got ten pence ready, waiting until I hear the pips. 'Alright, big man. What you up to? Want to go to the game? Aye, I'm on my way to work now, but don't worry, I'll think of something. Brilliant. See you soon, Bobby.'

I have two options. Three if I consider doing nothing. But doing nothing isn't a practical option today. I can wait until after tea break, stick fingers down my throat to encourage the re-emergence of my rolls and square sausage, then dutifully inform the manageress I'm too ill for work and have to go home.

Or I can be honest and tell her I need to meet my Da at Love Street today, hoping she understands the importance of the situation to my general health and mental well-being.

'Sorry about the mess, Gordon.' My colleague's filling the mop bucket while I'm putting my jacket on. I hobble downstairs to the shop floor as if I'd came second best in a fifty-fifty with Roy 'Feed The Bear' Aitken. 'Thanks for letting me go home, Christine. It must've been something I ate. I'm sure I'll be okay for Monday.'

She's too busy ushering customers around the pile of sick at the checkout to pay much attention to my pantomime performance.

Once out of sight from the shop my resurrection is complete and I head into Ahmed's for a packet of Rizla and a few cans of Tennents for the train.

I've only been to Love Street once before. 11th October 1980. An unremarkable game probably not remembered by many. Celtic won 2-0 on their way to winning the title that season.

That game stands out for me as it's the last one I attended with my Da. At the time I was thirteen and usually made my own way to games with mates. I only got to Love Street that day because my five year old brother, who my Da took to the games after I became too big for a lift over the turnstile, was ill.

Sitting with a can in my hand I keep a low profile on the train to Paisley. I do a bit of foot tapping as I look out the window but I'm not yet ready to go Roamin' in the Gloamin' or March with O'Neill. Bobby is belting out tunes with a donkey-hoarse voice. He gives me a wink with the 'Oh it's good to be a Roman Catholic' line, even though he's a Protestant. Industrial wastelands whiz past quicker than Jimmy Johnstone on the wing and I wonder if my Da will be at the game today. Of course, he'll be there. He couldn't miss a day like today. He's a man of faith. Maybe he can pull a few harp strings with the big fella to swing it in our favour.

The train slides into the station and I look for where we can build a couple of joints and buy another few cans and half bottle of Eldorado. It's at least a fifteen minute walk from Gilmour Street to Love Street so we don't want to get caught short.

We reach the ground half an hour later with drunken memories of a hangover and take our place level with the eighteen yard box opposite the

Main Stand. It might not be Celtic Park but today it feels like home. It feels like The Jungle. I have a quick look around but there's no sign of my Da.

My heart sinks a bit when the team take the field wearing the green away strip instead of the famous hoops but I don't say anything. I gee myself up.

'Come on the Celtic!' I shout. My high-pitched teenage voice drowned out by the roar of hope and expectation from the ever-growing Celtic support cramming in to the away end, the home end and with us in the middle end.

We need a miracle of the five loaves and two fish proportion but an early goal would do for a start.

Six minutes gone. Brian McClair rises above everybody in the box to meet an Owen Archdeacon corner. One down. Three to go. I can see a few punters with trannies to their ears. I don't want to know what's happening at Dens Park yet. Let's get our job done first.

'Come on the Celtic! Get into this fuckin' mob!'

Thirty minutes gone. Still one nil. We're playing alright, but we need goals more than we need silky fitba. Still no news from Dens.

Paul McStay finds Maurice Johnston in acres of space. 'Come on, wee man!'

Two down. Two to go. I don't want to think about it too much, but can't help it. We might just do this.

Danny McGrain, still one of the world's most attack-minded full-backs, is in our box facing Paddy Bonner with two St Mirren players closing him down. Somehow he hits the ball over his shoulder straight to Murdo McLeod on the edge of the box. Murdo lays off a first-time ball to Danny who's already turned and on the move forward. 'Go on Danny! I shout. He plays a first-time pass to Paul McStay who's popping-up everywhere wanting the ball. Paul cuts inside and looks up for options. Look at Danny, he's still overlapping down the right. Roy Aitken gathers the ball from Paul and passes to Danny who's now in the St Mirren half. Another first-time pass from Danny down the line finds Brian McClair. With a gallus flick he nutmegs the incoming St Mirren defender and lays an inch-perfect pass to Johnston in the box. Mo finishes with his first touch. Sublime.

I'm pushed forwards and sideways and settle on a safety barrier several steps down, there's a roar in my ear and I'm hoarse from shouting. I'm jumping about hugging people I don't know. I look for Bobby to tell him that's the best team goal I've seen Celtic score, and one of the best goals ever, but I can't see him. He's lost in his own huddle elsewhere.

Another part of me begins to believe. We're the Pope's eleven. We can do this.

Great run by Archdeacon. Paul McStay skelps it into the top corner with the outside of his boot. That's the all-important fourth goal, and it's not even half-time.

Celtic have done what they had to do, and done it in a style worthy of champions. I find Bobby and shout at him above the bedlam: 'Fuck sake. If we played like this every week the league would've fuckin' been won last month.'

At half time we go for a pee and finish the wine, and reality sets in. Dundee aren't doing the business for us at Dens; it's still nothing each with Hearts over there. I feel a whitey coming on but I'm not sure if it's the interval joint or nerves about what's going on at Dundee.

As the second half begins the players on the park seem to have eased up but it doesn't stop us adding another. I jump up, but it's a bit half-hearted now. 'Well done Brian McClair,' I say to the old guy next to me and nobody in particular. 'That fifth gives us a bit of a cushion, just in case St Mirren sneak a fluky one.'

Torrential rain starts. It's an omen of sorts. It must be. Thank God I'm not behind the goals today, or in the enclosure under the Main Stand where I stood with my Da on our last game together. That's probably where he'll be. My head's fair spinning now.

Our Father, who art in Heaven Hallowed be thy name...

Right, fuck that. It's too early for the prayers. I look about in front of me for inspiration, a sign even. A small group of older men who look in a worse state than me burst into a wee chorus of my Da's favourite song.

Oh Hampden in the sun,

Celtic seven Rangers one.

All my days I will sing in praise

of the Celtic team that played the day.

I join in the singing as if I'm joining my Da, my thoughts drifting backwards-- him telling me how, on his way back from the League Cup Final in 1957, an eager Rangers fan noticed my Da's colours, and approached him to ask about the score. This was during a period when Celtic were not at their best, so there was more than a hint of confidence about the request.

With a straight face my Da informed him Willie Fernie scored for Celtic with a last minute penalty.

'Jammy bastards,' the man said.

'Aye, jammy bastards alright, that only made it seven. It should've been more,' came the punch line.

The song dies out and my attention is drawn back to the park. The rain is running off the terracing roof above us but we're snug enough where we stand. Nothing much is happening on the pitch. The only thing moving is the clock and my head when I shut my eyes. There might as well be a wee guy walking around the track wearing a 'The End Is Nigh' sandwich board. I've got a bad feeling but I don't want to share it.

I can hear someone behind going on about how we lost the league at the Aberdeen game or the Rangers game. I turn around and tell him to shut up, the league isn't lost yet.

'Come on Dundee!' an old guy next to me shouts.

He's steamin' right enough. I join in. 'Do something for fuck sake!'

The St Mirren fans know it's hopeless. They've been well gubbed, but for the first time today they start singing – The Sash. Normally, we'd accept the challenge right away, but today it's like fog in the brain. A half-hearted chant is flung in their direction, before grumbling away to dirty bastardin' silence. Even the police patrolling the ground are smiling.

I wish I had a bloody radio. I can't even see those I seen with one earlier.

Something's happening. Pockets of fans around the ground are erupting. It must mean...it can only mean...surely to God.

I'm jumping, I'm up in the air scrambling forwards, somebody has their arm round my neck, somebody is kissing me on the forehead but I still don't know why. My mind's telling me something I can't allow myself to believe. Not without proof. Like a doubting Thomas I need to see or hear it for myself.

The whole place is jumping.

Bobby appears from nowhere and grabs and hugs me. 'Dundee have scored! They've fuckin' well scored!'

The tears come, but I don't mind. And neither does anyone else. All around me grown men are bubbling like weans. It's a sight to behold.

We jump among the thronging, jubilant crowd; upstairs, downstairs, tears streaming down faces of men and boy alike, feeling part of something, something special.

Even the idiot who was moaning about where we lost it has become a wise man. He's greeting, too.

Fuck sake. I hope that's not pish I'm standing on. I've lost a bastardin' shoe.

Everybody's got an eye on each other, waiting, making sure that it's not a dream, getting ready for the final whistle. I'm hopping about trying to find a shoe worth a pound.

There it is, about five steps away. I crouch down, keeping my eyes on the prize. The place erupts again.

Instinct kicks in. I jump up and join the celebrations. I haven't a clue what we're celebrating but I'm certain it's not a Hearts goal. I'm hearing mixed reports. It's either full-time at Dens or Dundee have scored again. Don't care either way. By the time the mayhem stops I'm about ten yards away from my starting position, and fifteen away from my shoe.

'Come on, Ref. Blow your fuckin' whistle.'

Thousands of Celtic fans are flooding onto the park and the players are running for the tunnel. Bobby finds me and makes a grab for me and tries to drag me towards the park. I hold up my shoeless foot. He laughs like fuck and pulls a nip of a joint from his pocket. A few puffs later the terracing's empty enough to reveal my shoe. We scramble to join the Celtic fans singing in the rain around the tunnel, but by the time we get there the call has already gone out to clear the park so the team can come back out and do a lap of honour.

I scan the enclosure under the Main Stand for a sighting of my Da. I don't see him, but I feel him. I know he's here. He's here with his Da, and his Da's Da, and his Da's Da's Da. They all love Celtic. I love Celtic. If I'm lucky enough to have a son he'll also love Celtic. It's in the blood and, on days like this, the blood sings.

Soaked we traipse back off the park to where we started. But nothing can dampen our spirits. Not even this Chernobyl rain dripping off my nose. The team lopes back on to the park. They can't believe it either. The fans remind them.

'Walk on...Walk on...With hope in your heart..'

There's not a better sight or sound in football than Celtic fans doing You'll Never Walk Alone, but I can't join in, not yet. I've a smile as big as the great escape we've just pulled and can't get this other wee tune out my head:

Oh Love Street in the rain,

The Celts have won the league again...

God bless you, Da. You'll never walk alone.

Borne On Wings ('Henke')

John C Traynor

dark destroyer, borne on wings

born to let the people sing

swift to smite foes overawed

put usurpers to the sword

touched by genius, humble yet

called to greatness, greatness met

with the legends set to dwell

litany of 'Greats' to swell

Nordo-Celtic demigod

ranks in unison applaud

mighty hero, mighty deeds

of our dreams the very seed

warrior back in ninety-eight

when the hounds were at the gate

wellspring of a thousand thrills

fearsome 'Tiger of Seville' …

… dark destroyer, borne on wings

Lord of the Wing

Pat Marrinan

Jimmy McGrory assessed his Celtic reserves with diligence. In October 1961, he watched his second string take on St. Johnstone. McGrory puffed his pipe as the teams trotted into a near deserted stadium. Scout, John Higgins, spoke in high appraisal of the skinny ginger youngster. McGrory thought he looked more suited to schoolboy football than the professional game. He wondered if the lad could cope.

The lad turned the Saints fullback inside out, lay on three Celtic goals and scored the fourth himself. McGrory left his seat that evening and set straight to signing James Connolly Johnstone.

The team Jimmy Johnstone joined in 1961 lacked direction. They had some explosive talents coming through, but were brittle and often disorganised. Chairman Sir Robert Kelly thought nothing of telling McGrory who to play and who to leave out. The crop of youngsters had to be moulded into a team.

Johnstone's debut against Kilmarnock highlighted these issues. A useful Kilmarnock thrashed them 6-0. Celtic, though, fought to the 1963 Scottish Cup final. Few favoured them against a dominant Rangers team. But a Hampden crowd saw Celtic raise their game. They matched the bookie-backed Bears for ninety minutes and earned a 1-1 draw. Johnstone gave the Rangers defence hell that day, giving the supporters hope of ending a six year silverware famine. Sir Robert Kelly, however, told McGrory to drop Johnstone for the replay. Rangers won 3-0.

Jimmy Johnstone bobbled on the first team's fringes for the next two seasons but was a ray of light to struggling Celtic with his mesmerising skills and growing confidence. Though a fine talent, Jimmy had complex issues. Spells in the reserve side took him to dark depths where he danced with the thought of giving up altogether.

One occasion which bolstered his perseverance came against Hibernian. The Celtic reserves left the park at half time and the Hibs gaffer addressed Johnstone

'What are you doin', Jimmy? You should be in the first team showing those skills to thousands!'

The Hibs boss saw greatness in Jimmy, but then, Big Jock knew a player when he saw one. Both were woven into the legacy of the other as time dragged them through a near mythical journey. A journey entailing much more than football.

Jock Stein came to manage Celtic with firm beliefs on how football should be played. Attack-minded, team-orientated, entertaining and inventive passing-play pillared what would become 'the Celtic way'. Wee Jinky Johnstone was a lynch pin of Stein's side and embodied the Celtic mentality. He flourished, as did the whole team, under the paternal guidance of his gaffer. Stein's Celtic ended Rangers' dominance in Scotland and conquered Europe.

In 1967 Celtic became the only team to win the European Cup with players all from the same country. At the Estadio Nacional in Lisbon Johnstone destroyed Inter Milan as Celtic pounded them with an immortal barrage of attacking play.

Shortly after, Real Madrid invited Celtic over for the testimonial of Alfredo Di Stefano. Celtic won the game 1-0. Johnstone's performance stunned the Madridistas, who chanted 'Ole' as he glided between their lines. Yes, Johnstone's off the field problems drove Stein to the brink and back. He worked hard to keep his star fit and focused, and the pair had their bust ups. But Jock loved Jimmy and Jimmy loved Jock. They complemented each other's greatness.

Anyone who saw the wee man in his prime was blessed indeed. He remains in the eyes of many the greatest player they had the pleasure of watching. Formally acknowledged as the greatest ever Celtic Player in 2002 by a fans' poll, he stood humbled on stage. Old Stein era comrades and modern heroes like Larsson beamed as they watched him. Jimmy bathed in affection that evening. Many in the crowd hadn't seen him play in the flesh but chanted:

'Jimmy, oh Jimmy Johnstone! Oh Jimmy Johnstone on the wing!'

On 13th March 2006 James Connolly Johnstone lost his life to Motor Neurone Disease. The disease was too big for the great who cut defenders to size on the ball. The week after his death, every Celtic player wore number 7 shorts. His name was chanted throughout the game and sometimes still is. In 2009 Jimmy's Memorial was unveiled outside Celtic Park. It's Jimmy as we remember, mid-flight, ball tied to his toe and poised to pounce. Jock Stein holds the European Cup behind him. The words hang silent in the air between the statues

'What are you doin', Jimmy? You should be in the first team showing those skills to thousands!'

'Ah did, Boss! And by God we wir the best!'

And so they were. Wee Jinky Johnstone, our Lord of the Wing, played with a smile. He played for the jersey, or as he put it himself-

'Ah jist went oot there and done ma best.'

We Are All Neil Lennon

David Harper

Winning is not just achieved by kicking a ball

Every Celtic fan knows it's about standing tall

As the press peddle the line 'they're all the same'

Rangers we're not, you're Scotland's shame

Eyes of the world have been opened wide

All your sins laid bare there is nowhere to hide

Losing to 'US' you can't contemplate

Lower and lower you delve into your hate

No more we'll sit back and swallow your lies

Every one of us see right through your disguise

Inside there's a feeling that won't be denied

Love for our manager, our club and our side

Lennon embodies what we feel for this team

Easter we'll swell into one it will seem

Nobody can stand in our righteous way

No matter the result on this holy day

Only the Celts need answer this call

Neil we are with you, you are us all

Cheese & Onion McCoys

John McClean

Hampden Park in 1988 had the Celtic End, the Rangers End and ...The Family Section, which is where we were. My dad was a guest of one of our players so he was opposite me in the posh seats. I'm still thankful to this day I was with my favourite 'uncle'.

We were 1-0 down from early on but, like any youngster, I was easily distracted and couldn't even remember when Hearts scored.

In those days you were told to watch the game. I listened to the Grand National on my Walkman, climbed the metal fence and got worked up enough to join in the chants of 'Henry, Henry, drop the ball! Henry, drop the ball!'

Time was against us when Henry came out for a ball and, in time-honoured tradition, dropped it.

Roy Aitken collected it and shot. The ball ricocheted like a pinball before Mark McGhee tapped in the rebound. The Family Section Collective went wild.

1-1 with a minute to go.

Now the game had my undivided attention. Walkman off.

Within a minute my other 'uncle's' brother lobbed a cross into the Hearts Box.

Mark McGhee challenged Henry 'Drop the Ball' Smith and, yes, you guessed it, he dropped it again.

Andy Walker grabbed the opportunity and volleyed it high into the roof of the net.

2-1 Celtic.

Pure carnage on the stairs of Hampden.

Scottish Cup Final 14th May 1988. A brilliantly sunny day, as always. Cup Final Day is ALWAYS Sunny. Trust me. If you're ever lucky enough to get a ticket for a final get the factor 50 splashed on.

"We're meeting Big P," said my Uncle. "His boy's a bit older than you, but ye'll get on fine."

This calmed me down a bit. I have no idea how we got to Hampden but I had the butterflies for the whole of the journey. Even now I get a wee 'driving over a hill' moment at the thought of it.

My uncle picked me up, as he did for the Semi-Final. Once again my dad was getting wined and dined in the corporate section – a few rows away from Maggie Thatcher, sitting next to Anton Rogan's mum – and her clacking Rosary beads. Celtic fans waved red cards at Thatcher and howled, "Baldy, baldy bastard!" At Dundee United's Eamonn Bannon.

Kevin Gallagher shut us up by scoring an absolute peach.

I was almost greeting. It was our Centenary year and we wanted the double. Big P's son and me also wanted a macaroon bar, so as soon as we next heard the man shouting, 'Erza macaroons!' we were off like a shot. The adults were glad to see the back of us for a while. Their nerves were getting shattered. Anton's mum's rosaries weren't working.

Macaroon craving sorted I gave the match my undivided attention for the last ten minutes and, for the first time, started to feel the tension.

"Keep the Faith," my uncle reminded me.

"How?" I asked. "The game's nearly done."

"This is Celtic, son. Glasgow Celtic. The game's never done until it's done. Remember that. Remember the Hearts game."

I stood toe to toe with all the other unbelievers, looked up at him and nodded.

Mrs Rogan's son swung in a cross. Billy Thomson done a 'Henry' and dropped the ball, and 'uncle' Frank McAvennie headed it in.

Again carnage in the Family Section.

I'd never been to a final never mind one with extra-time or penalties. I was daydreaming about Billy McNeill needing a player ... and asking me to take the winning pen.

The ball was centred. Game on again. The ghosts of Celtic past must be looking after us.

There wasn't any more than a minute to the final whistle when we won a corner.

I was thinking – No way? Can we? He did say 'Keep the Faith.'

Joe Miller passed the corner to the edge of the 18 yard box. Billy Stark sclaffed the shot goal bound. The ball pinged about all over the place before ending up at 'uncle Frank'.

He shot. He scored.

That proved to be the winner and delivered the double in our centenary year.

TOTAL BEDLAM IN THE FAMILY SECTION.

That was my first experience of hugging strangers. Total strangers lifting me in the air.

Screams of 'unbelievable' and 'lap it up wee man' and 'ya fuckin beauty' rang in my ears.

My uncle had a sly dig at his brother not having as much fun 'over there' in the posh seats.

We finally left Hampden after cheering every player that lifted the Scottish Cup. The only one we booed was Thatcher.

As we headed for the train we stopped at RS McColls and my uncle offered to get me a packet of crisps for the train home. "Any kind .. go for it. In fact, have two packs."

I usually wasn't allowed McCoys because they cost 55p a bag. "Really? Two packets Uncle T?" Those Cheese and Onion McCoy's were the best packets of crisps I've ever had.

Heaven's Roar

J J Whelan

God created a football team

Home turf being in heaven

Team of champs he did require

Selected his first eleven

John Thomson stands secure in goal

Tully, McStay and Johnny Doyle

Tommy Burns and Phil O'Donnell

Craft their skills on hallowed soil

Jimmy McGrory and Willie O'Neill

Jimmy Johnstone the best we've seen

Joe McBride and Bobby Murdoch

Managed by The Great Jock Stein

No corruption up in heaven

As GOD is the referee

No silly transfer fees

As everyone's for free

If you hear thunder from above

It's those angels in the crowd

When that ball does hit the net

They stamp their feet so loud

We all have angels in that crowd

Who again someday we'll meet

Let's pray the team keeps scoring

And fond memories we'll keep

The Big Cup

Jack O'Donnell

Da bangs the front door shut and the metallic pre-fab walls vibrate. Crawling from sticky linoleum in the kitchen to the jobby-brown carpet in the living room I'm pretending to be a snake. Da steps over me. His eyes scan the living room. It's a face looking for clues, a body in a hurry. He ganders into the kitchen. The plastic basin is placed on top of yesterday's Daily Record, filled with boiling water for his feet. A clean but threadbare cream colour towel lies on the back of the chair. Mum's sitting side-saddle on the other kitchen chair, facing the door and Da, cleaning Bryan's face with the edge of a lollipop-red dish cloth imprinted with the map of Africa. Bryan tries to squirm away, but she clasps his pudgy little arm and chuckles at the contortions of his face, the little gasps and the limb-thrown fury, as if he's being rubbed out. She kisses the crown of his hair, lifts him onto the floor and eases up out of the chair with a sigh, to get Da's dinner. Potatoes, turnip and mince, the same meal we got for our dinner, simmers in separate pots on three of the four rings that work. He trails shipyard smells of dust and oil which fills the kitchen and flings himself into his waiting seat, unties the unmatched string of his laces and kicks off gnarled work boots. His wool socks are darned at the heel with blue wool that doesn't match. He's a great man for the darning, crouched, head tilted as if listening to the wool and the sock tight against a circular glint of a Vaseline tin. He arches his foot to exercise witchery-tinged toenails, rolling up both trouser legs and his splashing fungal-white feet break the shine of the water. He scrubs at the sole and between his toes with a sliver of hard orange-yellow soap. The reek of carbolic fills my nostrils and I taste it on my tongue. Bryan makes a frog jump towards me and sits on my back as I slither. A creasing of the forehead and beetling bushy eyebrows from Da as he turns to look at us makes me consider growing feet.

'Enough of your nonsense.' He warns me. He warns us. 'Get in there and behave yourself.'

I leap up, standing at the kitchen door, just out of range of swinging hands that fetch you a skelp. Bryan holds onto my legs. I pat him on the head. He's too wee to understand. 'Sshh,' I whisper to him.

'I went for a quick pint of Guinness with McBride.' Da tells Mum.

Mum's got a fag in her mouth now. She's got the rings turned up full, stirring the mince with a spoon and holding her fag away to savour it

'Big game tonight.' Da runs the towel between each toe and wipes at the soles of his feet. He splays and curls up his toes like an upside down crab to keep them clean as he carries the basin the few steps along the tiled stone floor, sloshing the dirty water out into the smaller of the two sinks at the window.

'I'm sure we'll win.' Mum tastes the mince again. Sometimes she doesn't bother with dinner.

'Ah'm no' so sure.' Da cups his hands under the cold water and splashes water on his face. He wipes at his mouth and chin and feels round the contours of his face, opening and shutting his mouth like a wooden puppet, working his jawline, as if deciding whether he should shave. Da calls people that don't shave dirty buggers. But he doesn't shave. He just rubs up and down his arms with cold water, sniffs under his oxters and, feet planted on the floor, turns round and grabs for the towel. He looks at me and I dart into the living room and Bryan follows giggling and clutching at the back of my white t-shirt.

Da hovers at the kitchen door. I rush across and sit on the comfy seat beside the living-room window. Bryan trails behind and tries to humph up on the cushions beside me, but I pluck his fingers off and he starts girning.

'Enough! Whit did ah tell you about your carry-on?' Da frames the door of the kitchen and living room.

Bryan starts his bawling and rushes by him, through to the safety of Mum's skirt. I sit straight-backed, my feet propped over the edge of the cushion, looking at the telly, but there's nothing much on – a man with a microphone talking about football. Stephen scuttles from the chair near the fire to the three-seater couch beside the door to the hall. Da takes a deep breath and sighs before traipsing towards the telly. He hunkers down and adjusts the dial on the telly. Grey snow flickers with a static sound then the picture flickers back to what it was. He's not satisfied and makes a grunting noise. He whirls round to Stephen. 'You been playing with this telly?'

'Ah've no' touched it. Honest Da.'

Da looks at me, but he knows I'm not interested in the telly. I'd rather be out playing hide and seek, or football, or lining up plastic soldiers and Indians in gigantic battles that involve the rocky mountain rug and the fireplace fortress, with sneaky-deaky soldiers with flame throwers hiding inside Mum's ashtray, which is kinda cheating, but somehow I always win.

'Time for your bed.' Mum shouts through to me.

She's got Bryan by the hand and she's pulling his little navy top off, with the anchor insignia.

'Och Mum!' I shout back, but my heart isn't really in it.

Mum's slippers slap on the kitchen floor, quietened by carpet, goes into the cupboard behind the boiler for Bryan and my pyjamas. 'Just five more minutes.'

'Just let the boy watch the game.' Reaching across to the mantelpiece from his chair, Da picks up a pair of black rimmed specs and they slide down the edge of his long nose and perch on the bulbs of his hairy nostrils.

'We'll see.' Mum snecks the cupboard door shut. She's my pyjamas in her hands and Bryan's. She takes him by the hand into the room first.

I out-stare the telly, not turning my head, waiting for her to return, as if that will influence her decision.

Stephen's bum's sliding off the settee. Clutching his fists he groans and smacks himself in the head when the other team scores from a penalty. Da shuts his eyes and his head twists one way then another, his nostrils flare and he snorts like a runaway horse. He leans forward when the game restarts as if he's trying to get his head inside the telly.

'Nighty night.' Mum stands at the living room door, with Bryan clean as a pencil in his pyjamas after having a bath, waiting for a response.

My eyes twitch sideways, scared of being captured and roped into going to bed. Da shakes his head and tugs at the lobe of his ear. Stephen glances at Mum and Bryan and locks his eyes back on the telly. He frowns like Da and sneers when John Clark kicks the ball out of the park.

Mum comes back about ten minutes later. I feel her eyes eating into me. Bryan doesn't like being in the bedroom himself. He likes to snuggle in beside me. I gawp at the screen. If I was Jimmy Johnstone I'd just get the ball and slalom past everybody and score a great goal. But he doesn't. He loses the ball to the dark shirts and Da moans.

'Sufferin' Jesus,' he cries, when the game doesn't restart right away because the evening news is on, 'is there no' enough sufferin' in the world, without them doin' this to us noo.'

The second half is faster. Tommy Gemmell is at the edge of the box. He scores. No chair can hold him. Da jumps up, his two fists clenched pummelling the air. 'Yesssssss.'

Stephen jumps about like a loony and I giggle.

Da's forgot to eat. Mum brings in his dinner. She puts a dish towel on Da's lap and hands him the plate. My plan's working. Give the ball to Jimmy and we'll score. Da's frowning. He eats robotically, spooning potato from the edge of his knife to plate and his Adam's apple goes up and down as he swallows. Then it happens. The ball breaks. Da flings the dinner plate up on the air and potatoes, turnip and mince hits the rectangular- white-Styrofoam tiles on the ceiling and finds gravity. It's black and white on the telly, but a glorious mess of bouncing colour on the carpet.

'Goal!' Da skyrockets up out of the chair.

'Goal!' Stephen springs into the air.

'Goal?' I smile to myself.

'There's not a prouder man on God's earth than me,' says Jock Stein in the interview later, but Mum's lifting me and dragging me to bed, to dream.

Glesga Love

Pat Marrinan

Ah know I've hud a bevy

but the things I say ur true

I've been oot wi loadsa burds

but nane as nice as you

Ye wur gallus at the dancing

Ye really turnt ma heid

and a bet yer papped oot boyfriend

wishes he wiz deid

But whit I'm trying tae tell ye hen

And it's no said as a dare

But ye know how ah luv the selik?

well ah fuckin love you mer.

A European Night to Remember

Craig D

Everyone with Celtic at heart understands how special European football at Celtic Park can be. Over the years we've had some spine tingling, jaw-dropping nights under the floodlights against almost every European-football powerhouse.

Whenever we speak of great European nights, some supporters older than myself recollect memories of Partizan Belgrade, a Cup Winners Cup tie which saw Celtic score 5 (4 scored by Dariusz "Jackie" Dziekanowski) at home but still knocked out of the competition with an aggregate score of 6-6.

I mention the Partizan game because, before the game I'm about to discuss, we had another nail- biting European tie against Tirol Innsbruck of Austria. Although Celtic would go on to win the tie 7-5 on aggregate, this was in doubt right until the end with goals scored in 87 and 94 minutes.

Celtic would go on to face Liverpool in their first "Battle of Britain" since 1983 when they were defeated 2-1 on aggregate by Brian Clough's Nottingham Forest.

This young Liverpool team were tagged by the media down south as "The Spice Boys". They had an abundance of highly respected, talented players such as Steve McManaman, Robbie Fowler, Paul Ince, Michael Owen and more.

As is the norm in these Scottish versus English ties the Scottish side was given no chance, which, to an extent, is understandable given the huge gulf in riches. So it was no surprise the media, assuming the tie a foregone conclusion, showed Celtic typical disrespect.

The build-up was different to what I'd experienced before. The media attention and the talk on the street were far more intense than Rangers games.

The atmosphere before kick-off was electric. The train to Bellgrove was packed-full of supporters singing. Walking round from the station to

Shannon's bar we bumped into some of the away support, which created a terrific atmosphere, with no issues. As a 15- year old I had the mistaken idea these type of games courted trouble, but as the fans sung together it was an absolute pleasure to be part of it.

I took my seat in the Jock Stein Stand behind the goals, close to the travelling support.

Both sets of supporters attending the game sang 'You'll Never Walk Alone'. The sight, the noise, the whole atmosphere was a truly remarkable experience, and what made it even more special for me was-- a Liverpool-supporting friend of mine agreed-- we Celtic supporters sang it better.

The game kicked off and, without having time to settle into the game, Celtic were already one goal down. A young Michael Owen scored on six minutes, his first European goal for Liverpool.

After a number of chances for Celtic, including a penalty shout, the Italian referee blew the whistle for half-time.

During the break I experienced something that brought me, a wide 15 year old lad, close to tears.

A year previously Scotland was shook by a sign of evil. Sixteen children and one school teacher lost their lives in the Dunblane Massacre. Like many across the nation, and further afield, Celtic supporters looked to provide help. Leading up to this game many forms of support were arranged by Celtic supporters for the Dunblane families.

"Every supporter entering Celtic's ground for the game against Falkirk tomorrow (Saturday 20th April 1996) will be invited to make a donation. Last year the fund raised about £20,000 for causes like children's charities, community action on drugs, and projects promoting religious harmony. About 100 representatives of Dunblane Primary School - pupils, staff, and families - will be guests of Celtic at tomorrow's game."

"Fans at last weekend's game raised more than £30,000 for the Glasgow club's charity fund."

"And Celtic bosses have said a "substantial amount" will be given to the tragic Perthshire community that is still trying to come to terms with the evil that visited the town last month."

Dunblane residents affected by the tragedy entered the hallowed Celtic Park turf and presented Celtic supporters with a plaque, thanking their generosity and kindness.

This show of emotional respect was enhanced when both sets of supporters again stood and provided another rendition of 'You'll Never Walk Alone'. Anyone watching this outward display of togetherness would be at a loss as to how the media could describe the tie as a 'Battle of Britain'.

It was impossible to contain the emotions and sheer pride of being a Celtic supporter.

In the second half Larsson hit a post, before McNamara brought Celtic back into the game by swapping passes with Burley and crashing a fierce shot into the net past James.

Celtic hit the bar and were again denied a penalty by the Italian official. The fans howled their derision. However, Celtic weren't to be denied and finally got their rewards from the spot when Larsson was brought down in the box. Donnelly smashed his shot off the underside of the bar into the net.

Celtic, the underdogs, were now 2-1 ahead. The atmosphere was immense.

As the end approached Steve McManaman picked up the ball just inside the Liverpool half and went on a mazy run, skipping past several players before curling a shot into the net. I initially assumed it was going wide and, embarrassingly, jumped up with arms aloft.

The full time whistle went shortly afterwards but the experience of a full stadium singing 'You'll Never Walk Alone' not once, but twice, will live with me forever. It also highlighted how Celtic, at home, in front of that crowd, are capable of producing a performance to silence the doubters, no matter who the opposition.

I See Tommy Burns

Lorenzo Wordsmith

"When you pull on that jersey you're not just playing for a football club, you're playing for a people and a cause."

I see Tommy Burns.

Every time I walk up the street, taking in the splendour of Celtic Park, I can see the man ruffling some youngster's hair, smiling warmly and chatting away, on show, his true engaging personality, his love of all people.

When I look out onto that hallowed playing surface, a surface that has embraced many a legend, I can see the ball hit the net after a most recognisable turn, running arms stretched out by his sides, fists clenched head back looking up at the heavens in sheer delight.

He's making his way, that beaming smile of sheer delight racing toward his adoring fans in those magical hoops, those moments of Celtic ecstasy.

I see his grit and determination when things are going against us as player and manager and person, I see him give his all, never changing, never forgetting what he represents or who he is.

I see Tommy Burns, The Man.

He glides with ball in perfect balance, caresses the pitch with spraying passes, not a blade of grass spared, his wand-like left foot, dictating play, orchestrating crowd, creating the tempo, the mood.

He floats on air, kisses the breeze, feels the passionate Celtic roar of love.

It's true no other compares his kind.

He is remembered as more than a fine player, for he is Tommy Burns.

He uses his body well holding off stern challenge, head up always in control.

He twists and turns, the magician offloads with perfect timing for a dashing run on goal.

He lights up paradise, scores his share with flair, never shirking responsibility. Remembering he is a fine, firm, but fair player is Tommy Burns.

He loves the hoops that surround him, as they love him still.

Every time I walk up that street taking in the splendour of Celtic Park, I see the man, I know we all do, we always will.

Sunday Afternoons

Kris Soal

Going to my dad's at the weekend is the earliest memory I have. It was what I looked forward to all week. Sunday afternoon meant only one thing.

You see, my dad is a football fan and being at his house meant I could watch, play, eat, sleep and breathe football. I need to be clear, though. My dad is not a Celtic fan. His friends say he was a Leeds United fan when he was growing up but he's long since grown out of that. Then, as now, he was a football fan more than anything else.

Sunday was our football day. We would go to mass and then head straight to the local pitches to watch Don Bosco's, a team all my dad's friends played for. After that we'd head home to the front room for some Spaghetti Bolognese and Football Italia.

Italian football was at its peak and players like Bierhoff, Ronaldo and Baggio were lighting up the league. I sat in awe at the sublime skills of these superstars, whilst my Dad sat and tutted and shook his head at every stray pass or wayward shot. After the final whistle it was back to the studio. Then the sound I'd been waiting for "GOOOOOOLAZOOOOO". That was my cue.

"Dad, can we go out and play?"

"Give my head peace will ye?"

"Oh please, you promised."

"Right, come on then."

"I'll get the ball."

"We're only playing up to ten, though."

"But Dad, we always play to twenty."

Our pitch was the driveway. It measured about twenty by four yards, was cramped with walls on either side, but it was my Paradise.

I felt like losing the Cup Final when my dad won. But when I won, which wasn't very often, it felt like I'd scored the winner against Rangers in front of The Jungle.

Dad liked to make up his own rules. For example, every goal he scored counted double or if I hit the wall with the ball he got a penalty.

Today's rule was different again. Apparently, I was only allowed to use my left foot. He claimed it would make me a better footballer. I think he just wanted an easier game. Strangely, though, this rule became a permanent fixture in the coming weeks.

Sunday afternoon, a few months later, and my dad managed to get tickets to the greatest show in town. I was finally going to my beloved Celtic Park. I still remember the butterflies when I saw the top of the stadium over the houses. I remember looking at the stadium, the Holy Grail if you will, and thinking "I'm in heaven". It was huge. He led me up to the turnstiles, up the steps, through my own 'tunnel' and there it was-- the pitch. I felt like crying.

When we watched matches on TV my Dad would get me to keep an eye on certain players during a match. It was normally defenders like Maldini for Milan or Sensini for Parma. Mostly to keep me quiet I think.

The team were out doing the warm-up and my dad said to me, "Do me a favour, son, keep an eye on the wee man there, number 25, do ye see him?"

"Aye, I see him Dad. What do you want me to watch him for, though? That's Lubo, he plays up top and sure I'm a defender."

"Just watch how he trains, will ye?"

"Aye alright, Dad." I smirked thinking my Dad had lost it.

"Did ye watch him?"

"Aye, why?"

"What foot is he?"

I thought about this for a minute. He was right. I'd seen him play plenty of passes with his right. But during the warm up he was playing 50-60 yard passes right on the money with his left.

"I dunno."

"See, son, that's what makes a great player. No one knows what foot he's gonnae go on. That's why you need to practice with your left foot. If you can use both feet, you'll be twice the player."

Sunday afternoon, two weeks later, I was playing for my local team. The match had been moved because of bad weather during the week. Being a wee centre-half, I wasn't much use at corners and never got much chance to go forward. Today was different. Maybe it's because I prayed properly in mass for a change. Whatever the reason, my team got a corner and I took up my usual place, on the halfway line marking their forward.

All of a sudden my boss shouts, "Take him with ye, Kris!"

"Eh?"

"Go to the edge of their box and take him back there with ye. If he doesn't follow, you're free."

"Who, me?"

"Aye you, now GO!"

The centre forward started to follow me but he must've stopped because I soon realised I was twenty yards from goal with no one near me. I genuinely thought my nose started bleeding.

The corner came in and was cleared, towards me. Without thinking I swung my left foot at it. I'd love to say I caught it perfectly and it flew into the net. Sadly no. It rolled down my shin and off the end of my foot, arched towards goal and nestled in the back of the net about halfway up in the corner.

I looked over at my Dad in shock. He stood smiling and gave me the thumbs up.

After the game I went running over to him. "Did ye see it? What a goal! Right in the top corner! Left-foot volley!"

"Aye, I seen it, son. Well done. It was a cracker all right."

"With my bad foot, too. That's all that practising. Thanks, Dad."

"That was all you, son. Practice makes perfect, eh?" As I walked to the changing rooms he shouted, "Son?"

"Aye?"

"Your wee man Lubo better watch his back!"

I was on top of the world.

Fireworks

Tom Leonard

up cumzthi wee man

beats three men

slingzowra crackir

an Lennux

aw yi wahntia seenim

coolizza queue cumbir

bump

rightnthi riggin

poastij stamp

a rockit

that wuzzit

that wuzthi end

finisht

Celtic's Unbroken History And Me

Gerry Reilly

Growing up in the housing scheme of Drumchapel, Glasgow, was a tough upbringing. Even more so, considering I was a Celtic-daft Catholic bhoy living in a street filled with predominantly Protestant families. Up our close the neighbours were all Rangers supporters who didn't mind reminding us of that difference.

During those early years the word sectarian never entered our minds. We just disliked them and they us. We were different and that was enough. Besides, we were better at football. That's all that really mattered.

Walking to school some mornings was a task in itself. I'd make my way up the street, passing oncoming kids heading to their non-denominational school. I soon picked up words like Fenian and Taig but didn't understand their meaning. Sometimes I longed to lash out just for the sake of it, but my parents always told me to be better than that by not reacting to them. I suppose this was my first real taste of sectarianism, but I didn't pay much heed. It was just how life was and everyone I knew also experienced it.

But no matter what abuse came my way it was never a challenge I shirked. If anything it made me stronger. My Catholic beliefs grew stronger than they may otherwise have been, and being a Celtic supporter reinforced the biggest sense of pride in my life.

Rangers striker John McDonald lived in our street at the time. He was idolised by our neighbours. Part of me wanted to be pleased for a local lad making it big but his choice of team made that impossible.

Our household brought a bit of balance to our wee street once or twice a year when my uncle Davie came to visit. Sure, the street may have had their 'John McDonald' but our family, and the wider Celtic family, had our very own David Hay. I'm sure you appreciate the obvious superiority I felt when neighbours compared him with John McDonald, or in any such exchanges throughout the years of the verbal school run. A member of the Quality Street Gang, along with the likes of Danny McGrain and Kenny

Dalglish, Davie also played in the 1970 European Cup Final and 1974 World Cup Finals in West Germany.

I used to sit on our living room floor, looking up in awe at the very same man who'd be standing in the Parkhead dugout, sharing stories with my Granddad about all things Celtic. From his time as a player in the Quality Street Gang under the guidance of the master, the legend, the world's best-ever manager, Jock Stein, to his very own experiences on and off the field at Celtic when he, my uncle, became Celtic manager. I cannot tell you how proud this made me. I cannot tell how proud it still does. I cannot tell back then how wide my smile was both during and since school. Aye, the verbals never really stopped, but the replies had serious weight.

My Granda and uncle Davie would sit into the wee small hours, perhaps sharing a cigar and a few glasses of whisky, burning the midnight oil. I'm sure to this day that my Granddad was just as excited and intrigued as I was, as a young kid, listening to the grand Celtic stories being told, for they were real.

My wee Granny had to close the living- room blinds as her front garden turned into a free-for-all rendezvous point for our congregation of friends when word circulated that Davie Hay, the Celtic manager, had come over to visit.

I never imagined such a small council house garden in the compact streets of housing scheme Drumchapel could accommodate so many people. Men, women and children, all trying to get a wee sneak peek and, if lucky, a wave, a smile or even an autograph.

Those memories are unforgettable; from the days of running the gauntlet of difference and learning the reasons why, days that have moulded me into the person I am now, to these days where I look back and say, 'You know what, I wouldn't change any of it.'

I'm now a father myself. My children experience delight on their frequent trips to Celtic Park. It's a grand feeling telling them about my upbringing and creating a bond between them and my Granddad. With pride we journeyed that same Celtic journey they do now. Celtic pride.

I know that, one day when I'm older or indeed no longer here, my children will sit and reminisce about the stories and tales, trips and games, players, managers and legends.

Like myself and my grandfather, and his before, my children will pass stories and tales of their own Celtic journey, steeped in a proud history of how they became fans of the greatest club the world has ever known, and how their own family connection to Celtic football club assures not only proud tradition, but eternal continuation.

Joe McBride

Paul Colvin

Born in sunny Govan, June Nineteen Thirty Eight

Two hundred yards from home were Ibrox's wrought iron gates

Though he started out at Killie, he was loaned out to Rob Roy

At 15 years straight out of school, wee Joe was just a bhoy.

He proved his worth at Killie and was sold for English pounds

But he'd unsettled times in England with Wolves and Luton Town

So it was back to sunny Glasgow to The Jags and Motherwell

Where he gave Scots clubs, including us, 5 years of bloody hell

Big Jock Stein was taking note and Joe lived out his dream

As his boyhood heroes signed him for Celtic's greatest ever team

These Lions played in Paradise with The Jungle as their friend

And Joe McBride will always live in the hearts of Celtic men.

Hat-tricks were commonplace but he'd gladly bang in four

And he carried on, relentless, no matter what the score

Fearless and a battler, he wasn't one to hide,

The fear of death faced every club, when the striker's Joe McBride.

He's mentioned in the same breath as all The Lisbon Lions

And would have been out on that pitch, of that there's no denying

Though his injury was serious, he was in that famous squad

As your op revealed a cancer, was that an act of God?

If he'd played in Lisbon, what would have been the score?

A debate that's still on-going with the only answer: More!

Inter would not have fazed him, they were just another side

He was a striker blessed with greatness, that was Joe McBride.

Respect and admiration, he earned while he played

And even in retirement those human traits have stayed

In death we mourn the striker and the man who gave us joy

A man's man, I've heard them say, but to me he's still a bhoy.

Paddy's Ashes

Pat Marrinan

Aunt Bernie intoned the last decade of the Rosary for the rest of us to follow. Once finished she and the other women filed into the living room for tea and a chat, leaving the men alone with Paddy.

'He was a good old guy, yer Da,' said big Malky, shaking me roughly by the hand. 'Great Celtic man tae-- never missed a game for years.'

Everyone associated my Da with his love for the green and white Celtic hoops. He worked for 50 years and raised a clan of weans in the Garngad but, for those who knew him best, even at his funeral mass, thoughts always returned to his relationship with Celtic. The night before his burial, laid out in state wearing his best suit, countless folk knocked on the front door to pay their respects. Some placed mementos in his coffin: a picture of Bobby Evans, a programme from Seville, an actual match ticket from Lisbon. On his lapel sat a badge with the crest of the team who'd played such a prominent role in his 75 years of life. Results dictated Da's moods, and his greatest moments of joy were those days when they brought more honours back to Celtic Park or skelped Rangers. Drink flowed on those occasions, as did stories and songs. After the women left we stayed to pay our special tribute to Paddy Brennan: Celtic fan, father, grandfather and one of the good guys. My brother Joe gathered us around his coffin, 'Right men, let's send Paddy off the way he'd want.'

To my surprise he began to sing...

'Hail Hail, the Celts are here, what the hell do we care, what the hell do we care....'

Everyone joined in and the words echoed off the walls of the late Paddy Brennan's home. He would have liked that. Later, as we discussed what to do with his ashes following the cremation, Joe sprung one on us. 'I'm going to sprinkle them over the pitch at Celtic Park.'

We looked over at him wondering if he was serious, or if it was just the drink talking. But Joe, in that serious way he had of making the daft sound sensible, was way ahead of the rest of us.

'I phoned them,' he told us, 'and they said no chance. But just try and fecking stop me!'

I started laughing but soon quietened down as Joe enlarged on his plan, which took about as long as it took to drink another can of Tennents. When he finished speaking he turned in a half-circle and viewed each of our faces as if waiting for objections.

'It might just work,' I spoke for all of us, trying not to let him see my Adam's apple bobbing up and down.

Next day we gave Paddy a send-off he'd have loved. St Roch's chapel, where he'd attended mass as man and boy, was standing room only. The funny stories of his adventures following Celtic brought laughter to many a tear-stained face during a fitting celebration of his life. To my surprise everyone joined in singing his favourite old hymns and, as the cortege headed for the crematorium, a large crowd applauded him off on what they believed to be his final journey.

Only a select few knew this would be his penultimate journey if our plans worked out.

The brief service at Daldowie crematorium quickly passed. There were more tears, but also pride in a life well lived.

Having shook more hands than a campaigning politician my brother finally returned to the funeral car with the urn containing Paddy's ashes. 'Wednesday it is boys-- let's make it happen.'

Wednesday seemed a God-given occasion for our final tribute to Paddy Brennan. Not only was it Celtic's 125th Anniversary but the highly-acclaimed best team on the planet, Barcelona, arrived in town on Champions League duty. Everything was set for one of those legendary great European nights at Celtic Park. We gathered about five o'clock at a bar in the Gallowgate. Joe clutched Paddy's ashes to his chest, toasting his memory. The beer flowed like the Spring melt of Winter, and the ice bucket emptied as doubles on the rocks provided toast after toast. Unfortunately, for me, as the designated driver I stuck to Coca Cola. The bar rocked and seethed as those in attendance drank and sang their hearts out. At seven pm we left the pub and headed unsteadily along the Gallowgate to Celtic Park. Crowds packed around the turnstiles in a late rush to get in before kick-off. Joe used the stewards' struggling to cope with the influx to his advantage. He smuggled Paddy's ashes into the Jock Stein stand under his coat, unchallenged, even though it was blatantly obvious he wasn't pregnant.

We took our seats and Joe, a bit the worse for drink, and a bit emotional, was actually talking to Paddy's ashes, 'See Da, nothing is gonnae stop us now, we're on the road again!' He scanned the yellow-coated stewards lined up along the trackside. 'Where is that big bastard?' he said, referring to a workmate on duty that night. We tried to help out by eyeing the stewards for him, even though we didn't know what the guy looked like.

'There he is!' Joe pointed towards a red-faced, young man whose thick neck moved right and left as he scanned the growing crowd apparently looking for my brother.

'You blind, ya fanny?' Joe shouted. He gesticulated and smiled before heading down to the front of the stand to exchange a few words with his mate. They talked for about five minutes before parting with a handshake. Joe quickly returned to his seat beside us to fill us in on the details.

'On the final whistle he's heading to the toilet at our block and I'm meeting him there. He's lending me his big coat and I'm over the wall with the ashes when it's quiet.'

An almighty roar reverberated around Celtic Park as the teams took the field and Zadoc the Priest, the Champions League anthem, blared out the stadium's speakers.

The anniversary celebrations, a momentous display organised by die-hard fans, covered the entire stadium in green and white.

Joe started talking to the ashes again. 'Ye see that Da? Fuckin magic eh?'

I choked up and hoped that wherever my Da was he could witness the spectacle and feel it. It was occasions such as these he'd talked about all his life. Joe, standing beside me, brandished the urn aloft like a scarf-- I felt proud knowing my dad was part of the show.

The game started and the atmosphere crackled in the chill November air. Then the impossible happened. A Mulgrew corner at the opposite end of the stadium from us was met by the onrushing Wanyama's head and the ball nestled in the back of the Barcelona net. Parkhead erupted like a green-and-white volcano.

'Yaaasss' roared Joe. 'Ya feckin beauty!' In his excitement the urn flew from his hand and landed four rows down. 'Daaa!' he cried, scrambling over the seats in the row in front of us. No sooner had he placed his hands on the next row of seats two-tiers down and he got hugged by a man still deliriously celebrating Victor's goal. 'Get yer hauns aff me fur feck's sake, I need tae get my Da' s...I need tae get my Da.' Joe pulled away, stumbling over another row of seats. I watched him disappearing into a mass of jumping and writhing bodies, his coat bent over, scrumming over the ground, trying to retrieve the urn. Eventually, the crowd settled a little and his face reappeared. His coat was torn and he looked more demented than usual, but he held the urn aloft like the European Cup, 'Yaaaas. Got ye Da!'

The game ebbed and flowed to its finale. Unfortunately, it flowed more than it ebbed, and the siege on Celtic's goal was like the Alamo at closing time, but the Bhoys were heroically holding out. Then the impossible happened once more. One of the world's best players, Xavi Hernandez, failed to control a long kick out from Forster. The ball ran through to teenage substitute, Tony Watt, who raced onto the loose ball and smashed it into the net.

Joe was hysterical and might even have mentioned divine intervention. 'Ye see that Da, ye feckin see that, that wiz fur you!'

Near to the full-time whistle, Joe headed for the toilet as planned and missed Messi's late goal and the heart-stopping closing moments of the game. When it came the final whistle was greeted by a mixed roar of sheer elation and relief. Nobody wanted to go home so everyone sang and cheered for a while longer. After about twenty minutes the stadium was fairly empty apart from the Barcelona fans and a few tardy Hoops supporters. At that moment Joe appeared beside us in a steward's yellow coat four sizes too big for him. We watched him trot down the stairs towards the pitch. Another yellow-jacketed steward, an older man, on the pitch side looked up at Joe and seemed about to say something and stop him when I roared: 'Here you, Specky! Was that no brilliant tonight?' His curiosity was sparked enough to momentarily distract him. After hopping the barrier Joe confidently walked onto the hallowed turf. He made his way towards the middle of the park and stopped on the centre-circle spot.

Just then the players and trainers of Barcelona returned to the field to begin their post-match warm-down. Joe cautiously watched them approaching before unzipping his oversized coat and taking out the urn. One of the players, Andre Iniesta, noticing Joe's Celtic scarf hanging under the coat, looked at him quizzically.

Joe unscrewed the urn and shouted sideways to the player, pointing to the container, 'Here, wee man, this is wan of the best guys that ever walked the feckin earth.'

The gifted midfielder looked at him and shrugged, not understanding either the language Joe spoke or the gravity of the situation. But when Joe slowly shook the ashes onto the centre-circle the little Catalan seemed to comprehend exactly what was going on.

Joe looked at the small pile of ashes as they began to scatter and play in the chill November wind. 'There ye go Da, I'll see you in a better place.'

Iniesta stood watching Joe from ten yards away and nodded with a smile before blessing himself—'Padre, de Hijo y de espiritu santo' — and jogging off to the other side of the pitch to complete his warm down with team mates.

Paddy was home in Paradise and Joe was a happy man.

Saturday Ritual

J J Whelan

We stroll along to Fallon's bar

Watching our Da's go in for a jar

We stand excited, awaiting the bus

"Big Bish" at the helm to navigate us

The London Road, destination to be

With songs of "Celtic" and "Over the Sea"

Spirits are high (if you know what I mean)

People all ages wrapped up in the green

Paradise in sight and no entrance fee

Praying by chance, we'd get in for free

With hopes of a double-up, or a lift over

A sea of green and white, and four leaf clover

We race to the "Jungle" to take our places

Two cans on our feet just to see their faces

Johnstone, Lennox all there to be seen

Forever blessed for wearing the green

Watching grown men with tears in their eyes

As they watch their team chasing the prize

Deafening chants, "You'll Never Walk Alone"

An uncanny chill runs down my backbone

A similar sight you'll witness today

A little more civilized in lots of ways

Businessmen, families and "Ourselves Alone"

With that same chill running down your backbone

Now things have changed in this modern day

Seats, fast foods and "Systems We Play"

We've had our moments when trophies were slim

But never forget our pride being a "TIM"

Another Planet

Stephen O'Donnell

They're no happy these bastards, are they, unless they're giein every one ay us grief? This game's been switched to an early kick-off in a misguided and, I think it's fair to say, unsuccessful attempt to tackle the dreaded alcohol issue. Looks like it's back to the drawing-board wi their latest plan. This place is heavin wi Celtic fans, all firing into their Guinness, their alcopops, their expensive watered-down lager; you name it, they're drinking it, I can even make out one or two mid-morning spirits already being tipped doon their throats as well. It's all because ay the by-laws, strictly speaking you're no supposed to serve the bevvy before a certain hour ay the day here. What's the rule, 1pm...? Noon...? I doubt too many of this crowd knows or even cares, but that's how they've shifted the game. This is the solution the Polis have come up wi, in conjunction with the clubs, in conjunction with the media, in conjunction with the browbeaters at the S.F.A. Get them oot their beds before the fuckin post arrives. That way, they'll no be able to get a drink in them before they get up to the ground. That's the idea anyway, I'd hate to be the one who has to tell them.

The pub's busy, but every face is known to the proprietor and the doors are closed. Bus and social conveners wander vaguely about, shouting out names and distributing tickets. Everywhere people are laughing wildly and chatting anxiously, no able to shut up or stand still for two minutes. Which is a pain when you're waiting on your mate to come back fae the bar. Wee Coyler does well though, twisting his way through the odd 'Sorry, son', 'On you go, pal', 'There you are, Martin' and arriving back wi three pints ay the Nigerian lager.

~ You don't want to break the law, dae you, but you're no exactly left wi much choice, eh? I observe, savouring the stout's bitter, creamy taste. God, I love this stuff. It's imbued with mysterious, revitalising properties, one decent-sized glug is all that's required to feel its immediate restorative effects. Just what you need after a Saturday night out on the ran-dan, chasing the Glasgow talent to all hours. At least it was Skelton that was daein most ay the chasing last night, I dimly seem to remember. He was treating aw the lassies to his 'I was a male model' routine which, considering the face Skelton has on him, takes a fair amount ay brass neck.

I told him, he had as much chance wi that line as his team had the day, and so far at least I've been proved right because I lost count of the number ay times he was hunted. Later on, I caught up wi him on George Square at Christ knows what time, slumped on the steps, waiting for a night bus. The seagulls and pigeons boldly helping themselves to what was left ay his pie supper. When the bus finally arrived he wasny for moving, so I just had to leave him there. Let's hope his bad luck continues for a few more hours yet.

~ You're no breakin nuhin, Coyler informs me. ~ It's him that's serving you. ~ Is that right?

~ Aye. And he's covered an aw, it's a private event. There's nae cash registers open, you put a fiver in the glass for the cause, and that's it. I'm surprised at Coyler, there's no way a man of his calibre should be taken in by that garbage. Maybe it's just the time ay day and he's no fully into his stride yet, although I'm vaguely aware as well that he could be trying it on wi me.

~ What are you saying, Martin? You've no fallen for that old line, have you? The war's over, have you no heard? That donation you gied him is going right into his back pocket, believe me, I assure him.

I'm still searching Coyler's face for any sign of a wind-up, but either way he's no letting on. He's decided he's no speaking to me and is just quietly sipping his pint. I can't say I blame him, I think this boy's in pretty much the same state as me, he'll feel a lot better wi a few cans and a couple ay his loose reefers on the go. Just as well we don't have the McGoldrick boys here to remind us that, regardless of ceasefires and peace processes, the struggle for a United Ireland is still on-going, and continues to depend on the generosity of ordinary people. It's no that I don't agree. In fact, I agree completely. The Free State was only ever a stepping-stone in my book. But I cany be bothered with any ay that nonsense right now, there'll be plenty ay time for aw that later on. And the truth is, I couldny have cared less where Coyler's fiver was going. After last night and the heid I had on me, he could have gied it to David Murray as long as there was a pint ay Guinness heading my way. I swear, the bastard that started us on they double vodka red bulls has some serious fuckin explaining to dae, I'm no kiddin.

I take another big swally from my pint glass, and as I do, I notice, mid-gulp, that I've become locked in eye contact with none other than Jock Stein. The big man and the rest of the Lisbon Lions are smiling broadly down at me; so is Kenny Dalglish, Danny McGrain, Paul McStay, and there's the real King Billy - McNeill - holding up the European Cup. I know we have a tendency to go on about this, I don't know how many times I must have heard it aw myself, but that's the image which captures the high point of the club's history. Vindication in one photograph of the worthy ideals of the club's inception. Don't believe what the animals say, yes Celtic was unashamedly Irish and Catholic in its origins, and the supporter base across the world today is still drawn extensively from that community, but so what? It's only when that starts to become a problem for people that the bigotry kicks in. Way back in the nineteenth century the decision was taken that Celtic would only employ people on the basis of their ability, a concept the Huns were still coming to terms with as the twenty-first century hurtled towards us. Orange bastards, man. The thing is, they've nae excuse either. They cany trot out the old line about standards of the day, that's just the way things were back then, because all the while, right from the off, they had Celtic alongside them, conducting themsels in an appropriate manner. If the club I followed was indulging in those kind ay practices, checking up on people's names and backgrounds, rummaging around in their past in order to find out what school they went to, and refusing to sign players on the basis of their religion, then my attitude would have been quite simple - Fine, you do that, but I'm no gony support you. And I'm pretty sure a lot of other Celtic supporters, down the decades, would have felt the same way. The fact that Rangers managed to escape any form of serious censure for so long, in the light of such blatant and overt discrimination, only goes to highlight the complicity and indulgence they were afforded by the media, and other institutions and pillars ay the establishment. This country didny exactly blaze a trail for equal opportunities employment. I'm only glad that Celtic never went down the same route, because then the supporters just wouldny have been interested. The club would never have been special, it would never have grown into what it became, and McNeill wouldny be up there, haudin up the Big Cup.

~ There the bus, I nod, as the awkward big vehicle hauls itself into The Gallery car park.

~ Haud on just now Kevin. Nae rush, eh? Coyler tells me.

~ No, I'm just saying. Take your time, enjoy your pint. After you're done wi that, it's Tennents Lager aw the way, I laugh, holding up my carry-out.

One or two of the Lisbon boys have been in this pub. Willie Wallace is a Kirkie man himself and McNeill, Auld and a few others have all turned up here at one time or another for various functions and anniversary celebrations. Wee Jimmy Johnstone was always at his exuberant, inebriated best, one time he came up to my da and was shaking his hand. I think the old boy was a wee bit star-struck, all he could manage to say to his idol was, For twenty odd years I've been wanting to shake your haun Jimmy, and now here you are, shaking mines. I was never really one for that sort ay hero worship masel, but I suppose that's one thing I could always ask wee Jinky, if I ever see him or any of the other members ay that team in here again; what's it like having your picture sprayed over every wall ay this pub. It's some sight that's on display here, there are a multitude of images everywhere you look, no just of Celtic, but the flags and colours of many of their opponents can be seen as well. The effect is to provide a fairly well-detailed, illustrative history of the club, which only goes to offer a bittersweet reminder, given the team's present circumstances, of the kind of illustrious company that Celtic used to keep, and hopefully will keep again soon.

Not today though.

Millsy's pleased to see that I'm up and about and have managed to put in an appearance the day.

~ You get a ticket Garra, aye? He shuffles through the ranks with a broad smile on his face. ~ Well done! I wasny sure you'd make it.

~ I wasny sure masel, Darren, I acknowledge. ~ It was a last minute thing. I was up the house last night and the old man calls me to the phone. He's wantin me to speak to his mate Jamesy Gallacher, you know Jamesy, aye? I'm wondering what this is aw aboot, then Jamesy goes to us, Do you want to go to the game Kevin, right enough? There's a spare sitting here and I've nae takers. I'm trying to tell him, Stay right where you are Jamesy, don't fuckin move or dae anyhin, will you, I'll be right there. The old boy's just laughing at us, telling me to come round and pick it up if I want it.

~ He paid forty pound for his, Millsy points to a rather sheepish looking Danny Igoe. Danny's wearing a Celtic shirt with a big number 32 on the back. Across his shoulders, where conventionally you'd expect to see the player's name, is written the word 'COUNTIES'. I swear, following this club gies you a better understanding of Irish geography and history than you'd get fae any school.

~ That's no real. Couldny have been a Celtic fan if he took forty pound aff you, I suggest.

~ Fuckin wasny either, Danny confirms gloomily, but deep down I know he'd have probably coughed up twice that amount. I better no mention it, but all I paid was the price ay a few cans of TL that I stopped off and bought on the way round to Jamesy's. He wasny gony take them either, but eventually he accepted a four-pack off us, leaving me to keep a few tins back for the day.

~ We're heading out the now, yous coming? I think Coyler is starting to get itchy feet. He's drained his pint already and now he seems eager for action.

~ Aye, we'll be right wi you, Martin, Millsy tells him. ~ Gie us five minutes. I finish my drink and big Duffy, who guards the pub's rear entrance, lifts the steel shutters for us and we're among the first on the bus, settling into our seats pretty much right up the back. Coyler's in the row behind and I'm next to Michael McAleer, who we picked up in the pub earlier on. Young Michael was pretty much by himself in there, but there you go, that's what these ballots can do for you. He was pouring what looked like quite a tidy sum ay money into that fruit machine that sits in the corner. The wee twally ended up rooked, so I bought him a drink. I cany say I know Michael all that well, he was a good few years below us at St. Ninian's. Not a bad wee football player though, I seem to remember. I mind his big sister though, that's for sure. Nicola McAleer was a pure darling, and a dead nice lassie as well. Inevitably though, because of her looks and her roving eye, she was the subject of many a scurrilous and unfounded rumour. Big Tooncey was one who was always bragging that he'd went wi her, it's just a shame you cany believe a word big Tooncey says. He has a bit of a track record, does Toonce, when it comes to boasting about his exploits with Catholic girls, which he's happy to elaborate for you quite openly to your face, usually embellishing his sordid stories with all the lurid details that his twisted imagination can conceive of. And there's never any notion that he might be gieing offence, either to any Tims, or women, or anyone wi half a brain who might be within earshot of one ay his ridiculous rants. This is because for Toonce, his own prejudices are merely a watered down version of the much more sinister and calculated sectarianism passed on to him down the generations. The boy probably believes he's behaving like an enlightened new man, sharing a bit ay banter wi his Catholic mates, and in comparison to some ay his elders, he could well be right. You don't want to stand in the way ay progress, unlike his old man, at least Tooncey'll no think twice about inviting you into his hoos. With Nicola though, he had overstepped the mark. She angrily confronted him in front ay aw his pals, and he was forced to admit that, no for the first time, he'd been talking a load ay shite, claiming unconvincingly that he'd mixed Nicola up wi some other bird, from the opposite end of the attractiveness spectrum, who he had in fact copped off wi. I'm tempted to ask Michael if they still stay in touch, but I decide it's probably no a good idea. Young guys like that can be quite over-protective ay their big sisters, one false word here and I don't think I'll be his new pal for much longer.

~ I wish to fuck they'd hurry up man, Michael remarks, suddenly sounding a wee bit anxious beside me, as the pub gradually empties out.

~ Stay cool Mikey, I advise him. ~ I don't think we're gony miss the game or nothin.

~ Aye but it's the nerves, man, is it no? He suggests, plausibly enough. ~ Aw this sitting about before wan ay these games, it's bad for the fuckin nerves, man, sure it is?

~ It's no easy, I concede. ~ I'm in a similar state masel. I'll feel a lot better once we're three nuthin up.

~ I'd settle for that right now Garra, I'm tellin you. I cany staun aw this waiting aboot.

~ It's Mister 'cool hand' Coyle there, I indicate. ~ He makes you feel worse because he's that laid back, is that no right Martin? Coyler has lit his reefer and is standing up to open a window. ~ What's keeping them, Willie? I shout down the front at the old legend, Willie McCreery, as he drags himself, with a groan and a wheeze, onto the bus in stages. There's a famous story of how Willie, when he used to run the bus many years ago, caused a major panic up at Tannadice one time, believing they were a man short. He had everybody waiting about for forty-five minutes, trying to figure out who it was they were missing. Every other bus is long gone, all except the Kirkie Shamrock. They're still sitting there in the Tayside twilight, then some genius goes and points out to him that he's forgotten to count hissel. That's the sort ay thing that legends are made of round here, believe me.

~ Christ knows son, he says to me by way of an answer.

~ Fucks sakes, I complain, but I'm only letting off steam. Michael's right, it's no easy, trying to deal with the nervous tension before one of these games, especially the way Celtic have been playing recently, although Coyler's clearly mastered the art. I'm no sure how he manages it, but I take a puff on the man's reefer and pass it over, just as the bus is finally filling up.

A group of about six or seven come out the pub, laughing and stoating about, led by Eddie Orr and a crowd ay his mates. Orrie's leading them in a chorus of 'If you hate the fuckin Rangers...'. I'm still waiting on the day some guy goes, I'm no clappin, I've been meaning to tell yous, I quite like them in actual fact.

~ One or two of these are no gony make it in the ground, Coyler suggests and he could well be right. There's a few boys already starting to struggle and they've no even cracked open their carry-outs yet. That's what happens though, with these kick-off times, folk just get tanked up aw the earlier. Then after the game, it's a case of having aw afternoon to get as blootered as you like. That's how incidents start to spill out onto the streets, but the Polis are happy because most ay the bother takes place away fae the ground, even if their event has passed off in relative good order. It was the riots after the 1980 Scottish Cup Final, when McCluskey scored in extra time, that provoked the crackdown and they've no let-up ever since. Drink was supposedly the main cause ay aw the rioting, although I personally believe the 'Huns no being able to take a defeat' line of inquiry was worthy of further investigation. I'm no sure what scenarios, real or imagined, they'll be anticipating here once more, but we'll be herded about the place like cattle again the day. Of course they claim it's all justified, because there's no the same trouble with football crowds now as there used to be, but still, the Accident and Emergency departments of the Glasgow infirmaries will be busy again this weekend. But as long as it doesny happen live on television, in full view of a horrified nation, exploited every inch ay the way by pontificating media cunts, then the operation will be deemed a success.

The irony is, I'd be quite happy to walk through a crowd ay Rangers boys on the way to this game and as long as they left me alone, I'd leave them alone an aw. I know that by and large the feeling on the other side wouldny be too dissimilar, most Rangers fans are just ordinary punters. Fair enough, they can be a wee bit misguided and confused at times, no two ways about that, and they seem to have a fairly slanted view, a lot ay them, on certain aspects of their own history. But still, it's the full-time bigots I take exception to, no the ordinary guys that just go to follow their team. The authorities clamp down, blame it on football supporters, move the kick-off times, segregate the fans, because that's what authorities do. Without the perception of imminent all-out mayhem, their authority begins to wane. But people cany be bothered with fighting at football grounds, it's no the done thing anymore. Hooliganism was never my scene in the first place anyway, the idea of young working-class boys, fae different parts ay the country, battering lumps out ay one another at football matches, while their communities and their way of life, and the industries that sustained them, were being systematically dismantled by vindictive politicians, always struck me as a pretty counterproductive way for people to express themsels. A far better idea, it seems to me, is to try and foster solidarity between supporters of different clubs, because we have enough threatened common interests to be concerned about. These Polis cunts should be targeting their resources on the real troublemakers, no ordinary football supporters, who for the most part try to maintain a good-natured approach, despite the way they're treated. But no matter what happens during the game itself, some innocent young boy will take a battering the night, for nothing other than being in the wrong place at the wrong time, and there'll be nae sign ay a copper to offer him assistance.

Millsy's been watching Eddie Orr and Georgie Matheson with interest as well, and has noted our concerns. ~ You're mair likely to see a dead man wi a stiffy than you are to cut out drinking before wan ay these games, he turns round and tells us, emptying his can ay lager wi a flourish, just to illustrate the point. I cany argue, he's dead right, but he might have warned us. He has me spluttering my beer all over the back of the seat in front.

~ But that's rank though, is it no? Young Michael seems less amused. ~ Aw the bother you go to, to get yoursel a ticket for wan ay these games, and then some Polisman goes and takes it aff you at the gate. I think the boy can suddenly see himself being turned away from the ground for the sake of a few cans.

~ You'll be fine Michael, I assure him, as Orrie and his merry band stagger aboard. ~ We're awright, we're no falling about the place like that. I can understand where Michael's coming from though, because I've seen supporters turned away from Celtic Park for no particular reason dozens ay times. Harmless wee guys who were probably just a bit the worse for wear. But I find avoiding the harassment is usually pretty straightforward, no that I've no been fairly blitzed before the odd game or two. Aw you need to dae is keep your heid doon and wait in line, as if you're queuing for communion, that way you don't gie the bastards the excuse they need. Michael's only about eighteen or nineteen, so I continue to blether away to the boy, giving him the benefit of my broad experience, playing the role of the guy who's been around a while, done a few things, seen it all. He seems happy enough to listen, and nods carefully at my pearls of wisdom, which is pretty funny because I'm basically just talking a load ay shite to pass the time. Feeling a bit ay a buzz, looking forward to the game, cany shut my mouth. He's a smart cookie though, Michael, I think I mind now he goes to Strathclyde University.

~ Aye, he confirms sternly when I ask him. Touched a nerve there, it seems. I don't think he's that keen to advertise his student credentials, although I cany see how no. Still, at least he'll be able to sign us into Strathy Union, there's a few ay us looking for someone with a card now that Armie's wee brother doesny go any more. They clubs up the west end ay Sauchiehall Street are all dead studenty now, but I mind when it used to be ned city up there. We'll arrange something in a couple of weeks, I tell Michael, and we'll fire into some tidy student fanny. Michael seems to like the sound ay this idea, he's hud one or two ay they dolly birds himself, he assures me, and we agree, they're all sex maniacs. Except for one I bagged one time, who was nice enough looking but wasny much cop when I had her in the sack.

~ I'd have been better aff trying to shag a fuckin ironing-board, Michael, he's amused to hear me tell him.

We're underway at last and the bus is heading up towards the Stepps by-pass. Pat Kelly comes round to do a headcount, sharing a joke wi one or two folk, telling us for definite who is and who isny playing the day. I wonder where he gets his information from, because usually it's about as reliable as yesterday's Daily Record. There's no sweepstakes or any of the usual fun and games on these occasions so he takes his three quid aff us and that's it. It's not long though before the singing starts up in patches: Hail! Hail! The Celts are here. What the hell do we care, what the hell do we care? Hail! Hail! The Celts are here. What the hell do we care now? For it's a grand old team to play for... and so on. I really think they should be saving it for Castle Greyskull, they'll need their voices there awright. But no: Bring on your Hearts your Hibs your Ran-jurs, Bring on your Spaniards by the score, Barcelona Real Madrid who the fuck you tryin to kid, Cause were out to show the world what we can do. Somebody's clearly had enough ay this already, because they're waving a cassette about, which seems to catch the mood, and it's passed down the front to the machine.

That combine harvester song comes on, but rather than a bunch of Westcountry yokels singing about swilling cider, instead it's a soft, mocking Ulster voice we hear:

My friend Clive, he's in the SAS

He said a change was as good as a rest

But then they went and posted him way down to Crossmaglen!

He's praying to God to be in Wormwood Scrubs again

Oh I've got a brand new shiny helmet and a pair of kinky boots...

That's more like it. Taking the piss out the army, you cany go far wrong. Next, it's 'Sean South of Garryowen':

It was on a gloomy New Year's Eve as the shades of night came down

A lorryload of volunteers approached the border town

There were men from Dublin and from Cork, Fermanagh and Tyrone

And their leader was a Limerick man, Sean South from Garryowen

An absolute rebel classic. One or two boys are up in their chairs, looking about, singing. Numerous flags and banners and scarves have appeared and are now brazenly on display. We're starting to get into the swing ay things now and I crack open another can of TL and tuck in, just as poor old Sean South is being laid low by the oppressor's guns. Michael's trying to convince me to swap my ticket with somebody else. The hypo wee bam has found the guy with the seat next to his and he's trying to organise some sort ay exchange. It's all because he has this big tricolour, and he wants me to stand next to him in the Broomloan, hold up the other end, and shout some heinous sectarian abuse at forty thousand Orange bastards. It's a fine idea, I'll admit. A fine idea at the best ay times, but especially the day, because these cunts areny gony sit quietly and watch the football when they see us appear, that's for fucking sure. It's Frank McGuire who has the ticket Mike wants, and I can see the man's no that keen to part wi it.

~ It's awright Frank, never mind, I tell him, but Michael's no letting it go. I've nae idea where I'm gony be sitting the day and to be honest, I'm no really caring. I only landed this ticket at the last minute because Jamesy Gallacher decided at his age, he didny need aw this nonsense on a Sunday afternoon and offered me up his seat. There's a big discussion being conducted with Millsy and one or two others joining in, and eventually me and Michael have a couple of seats next to one another, although Christ knows how it's all been sorted.

~ Gony be magic man, we'll be right there, Michael tells me. It's pretty funny, this boy is under the impression that I'm some sort of big IRA man. I'm no sure where this idea comes from, I certainly don't propagate the notion, even on a day like this when there's a lot ay bravado and other high jinks going on. But Michael's no the first one to have bothered me wi this, the wee apprentice at my work was the same, he was always pestering me for information about Ireland, asking me loads ay questions, treating me as if I was the font ay aw knowledge. It's not something I'm particularly comfortable with in all honesty, I'm no like my uncle Pat, who was on the civil rights march in Derry on Bloody Sunday, in 1972. He was there, singing 'We shall overcome', on the day when it all kicked off, and there's no way he could be regarded as any sort ay sympathiser, so I don't see how I can be either. It's true, I've read Tim Pat Coogan and I know a bit about the history of Ireland, but that's no quite the same thing as being dragged out your house in the middle ay the night, or being battered by drunken polismen and shot at by soldiers. There's a fair chance that one or two of the family anecdotes may have sharpened my opinions on one or two subjects, and maybe that's what leads to the confusion; my auntie Rosemary, only just married, rushing out of their house up on Eastway in the Creggan Estate, leaving the front door wide open behind her, and running down to the Bogside looking for Pat after she heard the shots – the terrifying crack of the live rounds from the Paratroopers' self-loading rifles making an altogether different sound from the dull thud of the rubber bullets they were used to hearing on an almost daily basis in Derry at that time; then there were the letters which the parents of the victims received from Loyalists paramilitaries, saying that they hoped their sons would all burn in hell, an outrage only slightly mitigated by the fact that malicious lies were being put out by the army, claiming that the young boys they'd just murdered were all active IRA men; how the whole experience brought the community closer together in their fight for justice, and so on. But still, despite my relative proximity to some of these events, I'm of a different generation and living across the water in another country. So I always try to make sure that any opinions I hold are as fair-minded as they can be, and informed by books that are based on intelligence and academic study, no just naked sectarian self-interest, which is what you're up against half the time. I really should try and set Michael straight but the chances are, that would only provoke further inquiries, and there's no way I'm about to engage in any sort of big discussion with him right now. If he continues to look curious, I'll steer him well away from the subject.

But he's no, he's settled down now and looking out the window as the bus pulls up outside one of the most notorious Rangers pubs anywhere in the city. There's one or two of the blue uniform brigade parading about and, as well as the shouting and swearing, you can tell by some of the gestures and ridiculous posturing that's going on just how pleased they are to see us turning up on their doorstep. We don't hang about, that's for sure, we're straight out our seats, leaning over to the window, blessing them all, like the Pope does when he steps off the plane. Guaranteed to do the trick, that one. It's all too easy really, one or two ay them are already wound up like fuckin cuckoo clocks. Millsy's no shy, that's for sure, he's right up to the window, and he's giein them some right abuse, so he is. Then something goes smash at the back of the bus.

I never seen what happened but there's a lot of simmering anger coming to the boil now, despite the calls from the older heads at the front to keep the heid and no to lose the rag. The driver swings open the door and steps out to see what's going on and about half a dozen ay us are down the front and out right behind him, Eddie Orr stomping past everyone, trying to shove his way out and across the street, which isny easy, because the lights have changed now and the traffic's flowing round the side of us.

This big Hun is shouting across at us above the noise of the road but the stones are being flung from another direction. A group of five or six young boys are hanging about not far away, acting smart and looking guilty, but not daring to come any nearer.

~ Haud on the now Orrie, I tell Eddie. The driver's round the back of the bus, inspecting the damage and I point the young crew out to him. Suddenly we're after them, but the wee arseholes are sharp out the blocks, they track suits and trainers they're wearing areny just a fashion statement, and they've bolted it up side streets and closes, over fences and into buildings. I catch sight of one wee scally lobbing a bottle in our general direction and I tear after him. He's caught out in the open and I take the boy's legs, in the classic manner of the professional foul.

He takes a flying heider into the tarmac but he's straight back up again, staggering away to a big wooden fence, sliding along it, trying to stay on his feet while all the time I'm hovering just beside him. I cany make up my mind what to do, whether to grab the wee dick and frogmarch him back to face the music, or whether to just let him scarper. I take a haud ay him and fling him to the ground until I can decide what to dae wi him. I'm fed up wi these wee chancers trying it on by lobbing bricks, bottles, you fuckin name it, at our buses. It's no as if it's never happened before.

Then I catch sight ay the knife. It confuses me momentarily because it's been in his hand the whole time and if he'd turned round and waved it at me, there's no way I'd have been peggin it after him wi quite so much enthusiasm. My brain's trying to compute everything just a wee bit too fast, and I cany figure out what his original intentions were, but I'm glad he was left isolated because I wouldny fancy squaring up to a whole crowd ay these bams. Either way, there's no much he's gony be daein wi the thing now, wi ma foot on his heid. I bend down and retrieve the offending weapon from his hand.

Orrie and a few others arrive. ~ You got wan, Garra!

~ Wee bastart's cairrying a fuckin lockback, look! I announce, still genuinely struggling with the full implications.

~ Fucks sakes, so he is. Here, gie us it. Orrie takes the knife from my hand and opens the blade, locking it into position

~ Touch me, ma brother'll kill yous, a splutter comes from the pavement.

~ I knaw whit bus yous are on.

The wee toerag's no exactly giein himsel much ay a chance. Even if I wanted to, there's now nothing I can do to prevent him from suffering the consequences of Eddie Orr and Georgie Matheson. I just hope the boy is gony shut his mouth and no try anything funny, because I don't think he knows what he's dealing wi here, and at that age these wee idiots can be too gallus for their ain good. The big man has a haud ay the boy, he picks up his head by the hair and shoves his face into a pile of dog shite that's lying by a nearby lamppost on a slab of broken concrete.

~ Up you get pal, did you fall oor? I'm only trying to help you. Aw, you're doon again. Orrie continues to torment the boy, rubbing his face repeatedly in the dog muck. Then, using the blade, he starts scooping the shite into his mouth, face and hair, ignoring the squeals and sputters.

~ There's some for your big brother an aw, he tells him, the cruel pretence finally at an end.

Sirens wail in the vicinity.

~ Go! Orrie announces and he shies the blade as far as he can over a semi-demolished old factory wall and we jog back to the bus. One or two of the Rangers boys are just where we left them, still looking for all the world like they're dying to come over and start a big rammy, although to be fair to them, I think they just look that way anyway. A Polis car pulls up behind the bus and that seems to disperse them for some reason, the majority disappearing back into their manky wee hovel.

The driver's out the bus again and he wants to go and speak to the cops. This is unnecessary, folk are becoming restless now, because we're sitting here holding up the traffic outside one ay the worst fuckin holes this side ay the river. He's no very popular when he eventually returns,

~ Gony get us the fuck oot ay here mate, you shouldny have come by this way anyway. ~ That's fuckin three hunner pound damage tae ma bus, the driver complains.

~ So whit!? No even your bus anyway, is it? Just you drive the fuckin hing, Orrie shouts at him, which cracks us up.

~ Problem solved mate, wee bastarts'll no be tryin that on again, Georgie adds. I don't know if he's heard them but the driver's no gony argue and we're underway once more, with the recent turn of events being variously described and elaborated on by some of the participants. I'm being dragged into the inquest myself, which is immediately and vociferously underway, but I'm still feeling a wee bit too dazed and confused to be able to offer much insight, after such a close encounter with the big city's knife-wielding subculture. It's little more than I can do just to nod, shrug or smile at the odd reference. I sit back and check my watch - less than an hour until kick off. I empty my can ay TL and crack open another.

The Civil Sevillian

Richard Wilson

A cataract in mind's eye

Casts out its fly,

Across the eddies of memories

Baiting, coaxing, waiting,

Anticipating.

The catch of the day

21st of May.

Two river cities of old ports

One disused, drunk with rust

The other drunk

As a sign of trust.

Flash-flood recall

Breaks the opaque line

Off the hook

Able to revere

Our day on the banks

Of the River Guadalquivir.

Casting back to that Celtic run

Green and White shimmered and caught the eye

As schools of hooped angels

Wandered and weaved

Creating waves in their dramatic sea.

Sevillanos dined on the taste

Of a rare, raw joy

A mixed platter of delight

Amongst coral coloured trenches street

And

Calcada-ed beach.

Through the whole course of the event

Adding extras

When the menu was set

Smoked and caught in our net.

In that Caliphate

A Civil Sevillian awaits

Anticipates

For a time to taste

When Celtic rules the leagues of C's

And brings our foes to their knees...

Flowers and Football Tops

Marc F Kiernan

On March 11th 2004 we stood in the North Stand remembering victims of the Madrid train bombing. I looked over to the Barcelona fans hoping they wouldn't utter any dissenting shout. But that wasn't the reason for my black mood.

I arrived at Celtic Park with the mother-to-be after visiting my sick Grandpa in the hospital. Whilst there we chatted about Celtic's prospects in the evening's match, results and score lines, and his hopes to survive to see his first great-grandson that would carry the family name.

I stood in silent contemplation, with thousands of others, and thought about my Grandpa. When the referee blew his whistle to end the impeccably observed minute's silence a deafening roar exploded around the stadium. My solemnness disappeared immediately, not at the prospect of the match kicking off, but being present at feeling the first signs of life in my partner's womb. The noise generated by the fans was so great my unborn son jolted in his temporary home. I quipped, "Guaranteed Celtic fan there."

The match took me through the emotions of delight (Larsson) and anger (Motta). Thiago Motta and Rab Douglas were shown red for a half-time fracas in the tunnel. Javier Saviola followed them in the forty-ninth minute for a dreadful tackle on Alan Thompson. Thompson, however, had the last laugh, scoring the only goal in the fifty-ninth minute for O'Neill's Seville Lions.

We walked back to the car, chatting excitedly about our new Bhoy's first signs of life, joking about how he'd play for The Hoops one day and keep me in a pension. That night we stayed up late, talking baby-Bhoy stuff and me heading to the Celtic shop to buy The Hoop's baby-grows during my lunch break.

But next morning brought the dreadful news we feared. My Grandpa passed in the early hours. I volunteered to perform the dutiful grandson role by being at his home to console his partner and help out as much as I could.

She asked if I wanted a drink. I elected for whisky in his memory. We reminisced about days gone by through tears and laughter. Going through the drinks cupboard I came across many bottles of unopened ten, fifteen and twenty year-old malts that I'd bought him over the years (turns out he preferred gut-rot whisky). At the back I spied a 1988 Celtic Centenary Year bottle in a mahogany box with two Celtic-crest crystal glasses and thought it must be worth a few bob. Knowing my Grandpa's legendary thriftiness, I realised what Celtic meant to him to part with a portion of his life savings to buy this artefact.

His requiem mass was in the chapel off Muiryfauld Drive and the burial at St Peter's Cemetery on London Road. We played a playlist of his favourite Dean Martin and Celtic standards. Lowering the coffin to the sound of 'You'll Never Walk Alone', I smiled when I noticed his final resting place was against the distillery wall. We then headed to the Celtic Supporters Club for the wake where I chewed the fat with other mourners. They asked about my partner's pregnancy and pulled my leg about me handling being a dad. It was strange feeling. The more people tried to cheer me up the sadder I became that my Grandpa wouldn't be around to enjoy his grandson.

After a joyous send-off at the Celtic Supporters Club we headed home, sharing the usual farewells and promises to keep in touch.

The following morning I bought all the baby-Bhoy paraphernalia I could afford and drove to my parents' home, eager to show off my purchases. I was shocked to find a police car parked outside and apprehensive at what trouble, or disaster, lay inside. In the living room my parents were answering a constable's questions. After the police left my Dad told me they were questioning everyone who was in the vicinity of the Celtic Club the previous night. To my horror an appalling crime had occurred yards from us behind the clubhouse.

Later that day I walked up to the club, not to be a macabre sightseer, but to try and make sense of what had happened. The area was cordoned off and impassable to the public. I noticed a shrine forming, with customary flowers and football tops. I listened to the gossipers around the growing memorial. Everyone spilled tears on hearing the gruesome details. More people stopped in their cars and lay down flowers or footballing accoutrements. I looked at my bag and, giving over to emotion, pulled out and placed a Celtic baby-grow on the makeshift shrine, said a quick, "Rest in Peace" under my breath and hurried away.

After Grandpa's funeral I kept in touch with some family members and we attended a few games together as a new found brotherhood. When the season finished I decided to pay my Grandpa's partner a visit and ask if she needed any help.

She was grateful for my company and said, "I want you to have all the whisky, son, including the mahogany box. It's no use to me. I don't drink."

I didn't know what to say but my flowing tears probably said it all.

She informed me that his headstone was installed the previous day, and I thought it fitting that the least I could do was visit his grave.

I made my way straight to St Peter's. Standing at the graveside I opened the best bottle of all, the Centenary bottle. Placing the etched-crystal goblet on the headstone, I poured a "half" and left it atop in memoriam. I tipped the bottle to pour the remaining whisky over the disturbed earth, but stopped myself and returned the bottle to its crafted packaging. After a few salutary goodbyes and promises I walked out the cemetery, turning left at the gates.

I strolled up London Road towards the Supporters Club and turned into the narrow lane that leads down to the Clyde walkway. The familiar shrine objects came in to view. I removed the remaining crystal goblet from the mahogany box, sat it on the wet earth at the foot of a tree and poured another "half" into the decorative glass. An elderly couple walked by and I nodded in acknowledgement, whilst repeating the "Rest In Peace".

Mission accomplished, I turned and walked away with a renewed feeling of warmth. The auld yin would've appreciated my generosity in the sharing of the Celtic spirit, in more ways than one.

Several toasts were raised in my Grandpa's honour when the remainder of that bottle was duly quaffed on the night my Bhoy made an entrance.

Not long after I came across another flowers and football tops shrine dedicated to a young lad taken in his prime. I rushed home, grabbed a ten year old malt and a glass. Since then I've repeated the process too many times. Next time you see such a shrine have a look to see if there's a wee half poured for the angels' share.

The Day Tommy Passed

David Harper

Tommy twists, Tommy turns, we're going to miss you Tommy Burns.

From boy to man a true born Celt, your sweet left foot made opponents melt,

Your flame red hair, your razor wit, we're going to miss you every bit,

As player, as manager and as our coach, you served our club beyond reproach,

You showed us every single day, how to live and play the Celtic way,

You lived as you played, honest and true, you loved the fans and we loved you,

So we'll laugh, we'll cry and we'll make a fuss, because Tommy Burns you were one of us.

Tommy twists, Tommy turns, rest in peace Tommy Burns.

My Old Mercury

Stephen Monaghan

As a child I stood at the single-paned, iron window, gazing into the distance of night at the always, it seemed, foggy Celtic park during matches, before the hourly news came on and informed us of the result. I'd watch my number seven Mercury crawling up the hill. If we'd won songs blasted and windows looked in danger of falling out. Cheers of victory were relayed by supporters staggering off at our stop, acting like street criers, informing all within earshot of the result, if you wanted to hear it or not.

It began life in the 1950s, and continues to this day. When I appeared, and became aware of it in the mid-70s, it brought my father home from the Glen bar in Rutherglen. He'd bring home bags of fritters and various confectionaries to munch while watching the evening highlights of the day's game on those ever treasured family Saturday nights. He'd talk of when he and his father-in-law, my grandfather, did the same journey and recall great games and equally great sessions in the pub afterwards. It pulled on folk's heart strings and be outside the aforementioned bar the back of two on a Saturday. Men out for a wee pint would forgo a few and an afternoon in the bookies to jump on it, and head the few stops to see the Celtic on the strength of a rumour of a young player from the reserves making his debut and not to be missed.

The years moved on. The Glen closed, but my Mercury would still be rising. The family moved home but, by chance, it still ran past our new house twice an hour, giving us a wee bit of familiar comfort. Although living somewhere new we always liked a bit of the old in our lives. I reached the age myself where I'd enjoy a drink after the game. I'd be tasked with bringing home the chip-shop soul-food, and enjoy a wee sing-song on the way home. We did it for three generations, until we all moved again, not far, but off the route that meant the world to me.

After night games now, when I'm heading home, it sometimes appears before my own transport. I have a selfish urge to jump on it, and sometimes do. The eight stops I sit on the bus, I'm doing what we've done as a family all the way back to the 1950s. Alas, the crossroads comes and I have to get off and walk the mile up the hill, but it's worth it, because when you're on it nothing else matters. No one, bar me, knows what the journey means to me. It might as well be a time-machine, as the memories of my Celtic life flood back. The trip gets shorter but the memories always stretch back a bit further. Of course, this could be any person's life I guess. What makes it so special to me?

To me it's more of a journey than a route. When I first got on that bus I travelled through areas not friendly or welcoming to those who filled Celtic Park. Time and fate have moved on. Most of the people that hated us have grown older, moved away or changed. A few still exist but, hopefully, time will take its toll on them.

Where does the route begin and where does it end I hear you ask? It begins in a scheme where a boy called Jim grew up and, briefly, went on to represent our club. It then goes down a hill and along a street where a chapel stands. The fact that a man called Bobby, whose star shown brightest one hot day in Lisbon, was buried from there makes it ever so special to me.

It then carries on teasing you as you see Paradise in the distance, before it goes by another place of worship, where a man Called Brother Walfrid had a plan to start a football team, and a red-haired lad called Tommy grew up nearby and became Mr Celtic.

The bus ends in another scheme where one of Tommy's team mates called Frank grew up and also went on to cement his name in folklore.

The majority of passengers in the 1950s were immigrant stock, overspill of the slums of the industrial powerhouse that Glasgow was back in the day. Today's passengers are mostly people from other shores who have also arrived on these lands looking for shelter and respite.

But it's more than a journey, too. As it continues on it reminds me of the cycle of Celtic. From those early days of putting food on the dinner tables of the East End to the cosmopolitan club of today.

How did it affect me with Celtic? I love what number seven gives to the club. Great men like Jinky and Henrik wore it with distinction. On a

161

personal note I was most happy when a Southside lad called Aiden chose to wear number seven, and in the present squad a young lad called Dylan wears the same number. It may baffle some folk, and seem quite bizarre, but for me Celtic and my old Mercury go hand in hand. When I think of one I always think of the other. That is my Celtic.

Jinky

Paul Doucet

Backend September forty four, gey near the end o' thon Great War,

At Viewpark ower in Uddingston, Mrs Johnstone bore a son.

They named the lad, James Connolly, that's "Jinky" now tae you and me,

He startid growin' jist as planned, but ne'er gained mair than five fit wan.

A shock o' curly bricht red hair, a grin, an' chin wae dimple there,

But on this diminutive child, some bounteous, glorious spirit smiled,

A special talent'd, been bestowed, tho' genes for later ill wid bode.

When jist aichteen fulfilled a dream, he ta'en the field fur oor great team!

Then, mair he played and mair he'd show, set Scotia's fitba' grunds aglow,

Defenders groan as oor fans sing, the dazzlin' dribbler on the wing.

Frae week tae week he made his name, a superstar had jined the game,

The utmaist test supporters feels, is shawin oor rivals jist oor heels,

Wae lots o' titles in a row, Jinks helped keep Celtic hearts aglow.

The greatest thing that he could dae, wis show thae Rangers hoo tae play,

The Derby games, the greatest test, on different plain frae awe the rest,

My mem'ry fresh as yesterday, brave, gifted, glorious prodigy,

He dummied left, n' feintet richt, he nutmegged Greig n'then took flight,

Like a terrier, streaked awaw, then slowed a tad tae trap the baw,

Well Greigy, took 'im in the back, way studs up, tried baith legs tae brak,

Frae oot the crowd, an anguished howl, play on cried whistler,"that's nae foul".

Then Jinky landed oan his back, as "clogger" sent him our the track,

Tripped, n' hacked, n' kicked again, get up said ref, this games fur men.

Mair brutal play ye scarce'll see, assault wi' clear impunity.

Hard or fair, eye no sae daft, a "style" protectet' by the "craft".

The wee man's he'rt wis, Leonine, they'l no stoap me the bluenose swine,

They couldna catch him every time, he cut them up wae play sublime.

Dribbled, dazzled, body swerved, wae skill an' cheek an' ootricht verve.

They never knew what else tae dae, could no contain his skilled array,

Truth is, the contest wisnae fair, bemused defenders scythed the air,

Nay maiter whit they tried tae dae, they couldny stoap this maestro's play.

They tried his will, n' legs tae break, n' still he left them in his wake,

Jist five fit wan, ye huv tae sae, the best o' pure, n' brave wing play!!

His talents grew an' gained him fame, sine half the world noo kent his name,

Red Star Belgrade tae Celtic park, in Europe they had made their mark,

But, on that nicht the world wid see, wee Jinks, score twa and lay on three.

An' so in nineteen sixty seven, wi' Jinky's lions foretaste't heaven,

In Lisbon's stadium o' licht, like stars possessed we played that nicht.

The fitba' world stood back agasp, the Champions Cup, in Billy's grasp.

The fitba that wis on display, had ne'er afore seen licht o' day,

Frae o' that talent that we saw, wee Jinky, shone abin them awe!

164

If entertainin' wis the rage, his skills deserved the greatest stage,

But Scotland's game contained a flaw, that maist wad claim they never saw,

As Celtic, sprang frae Irish roots, subject tae bigots, claithed in suits.

The S.F.A. his face oft slapped, for, Henderson, maist got the caps,

A guid like player a dare'say, nae drawbacks like, wi' Celtic play!

Whaur's sic anither fitba' nation, wid no hae Jinky, at his station.

Law, Giggsy, Mathews, and the rest, there's even Belfast's Georgie Best,

For goad gien genius you micht find, oor Jinky left them awe behind.

Three hundred games afore we severed, confirmed as," Celtics Greatest Ever".

But, ony diamond has some flaw, oor much loved hero, worst of awe,

The mystery which brocht his gift, cast his protective powers adrift,

Whatever gave him talents wealth, sine never helped watch ower his health,

Too sune cam time tae leave this place, another team he noo micht grace,

Tae that same place his riches bring, for evermore he'll grace the wing,

Noo, if theres' fitba played in heaven, I'm share we ken whaws number seven,

The Importance of Celtic

Steven McGhee

I never considered writing about my condition, or about Celtic. Certainly not about the close link between the two. This piece came about by chance, like many, because after reading the story of another Celtic supporter I was inspired. Another domino in the chain that makes us so special.

This is first and foremost about Celtic, not my situation or my condition. It is about the positivity and emotion a team, only a team like Celtic, can inject into someone's life.

Slightly over five years ago I went on my best mate's stag weekend to Magaluf. Within minutes of arriving I impulsively decided that, despite it being 2 AM, it would be a great idea to dive into the swimming pool. Unfortunately for me I didn't judge how narrow the pool was and, at just the same time as I entered the water, my head collided with the wall of the pool at the opposite end. I lay floating, face down and conscious, until my friends realised I was not messing about and dragged me out the water. I knew it was bad straight away. Although I could move my head I couldn't feel anything below my neck.

I spent one week in hospital in Spain being operated on to secure my neck before I could be flown home and sent to the Southern General Hospital in Glasgow. I broke my neck at the C2 vertebrae which is only inches from the base of the brain. 80% of the time this injury would be discovered post-mortem so I can be included as one of the lucky 20%. Complications during the operation resulted in me losing the ability to breathe on my own. I am now attached to a ventilator 24 hours a day.

I stayed in the Southern General for just over one year recuperating. I was lucky enough that during my time in hospital a large custom-designed extension was built onto the back of my parents' house. Living in the same building as my parents at 30 years of age is not ideal but it does have many benefits. None more than some of mammy's home cooking.

I live with two carers at all times. 24 hours a day 7 days a week. This can be difficult but it is unavoidable due to the regular fluctuations in my health, the constant risk of something going wrong with my breathing and the necessity to have someone with working arms and legs available. Fortunately a number of my friends have been trained to a level that I can be left with them to enjoy my social life. I am blessed enough to be surrounded by a great family and loyal friends who I know will always be there no matter what, and for that I am incredibly grateful.

I am not going to dwell on the negative aspects of my situation or what I regret or dealing with pain. That is not important here. I just wanted you to have a picture of where I am and how I got here.

My feelings are what I really want to share. I am going to do this without exaggerating for the sake of dramatic effect. I will share my personal feelings and, in doing so, hope that I can, in the most honest way possible, describe something extremely important. What Celtic have meant to me and continue to do day by day.

Football has always been important in my life. I hold my hands up in admission that as a young boy my dad would take me to Rugby Park to watch Kilmarnock. I didn't know any better but I loved being squashed up in the terracing of the Johnnie Walker stand, strangers lifting me up to help me see the game.

It planted the seed and when I was old enough to know better I realised there was something special about Celtic. Something about the spirit of the team, the history, the philosophy of playing football the right way and sticking to that philosophy, even as Rangers racked up the (now tainted) trophies and league titles. Something about the fans. Recently a phrase has been attached to our current manager that sums all this up perfectly, "something inside so strong".

Something inside so strong. Everyone has it but sometimes we need to dig deep to find it. Celtic have been my go to place/team/family when I need to find that thing inside. Over the last five years the passion I feel for Celtic, and the supporters I am now fortunate enough to know, has grown, and that "thing" that makes everything about the club so special has become more and more important to me.

I don't feel guilty saying this and I mean no disrespect to my family or friends, because they are precious to me, but Celtic mean just as much to me as anything or anyone in my life.

I have my bad days. Christ, I have my really bad days. These are the days when it is easy to sit thinking about what could have been and what I have missed out on in life. As the years passed I have discovered something so simple. That concentrating on something I'm passionate about, for me that is Celtic, can hold those thoughts at bay. Seems obvious. I think about the special games, the special players, the special goals. I think about the team at the moment. What excites me about it and what I'm concerned about. I think about the future, where we can go and how much fun it will be getting there. It has taken me years but now it is a subconscious reaction when I am struggling

Many of you will be thinking "I think about those things all the time, too". When you can teach your brain to go to that place as a natural instinct to fight off depression then that is something special. That is something that needs to be powerful. I have tried the obvious "happy thoughts" that the psychologists in the hospital teach you to use. Those things just don't do it. Celtic Football Club is my thing. It is my barrier that protects me from falling into darker places.

Without being too sombre, I don't know how long I will be about. I suppose nobody does. I know my situation is precarious and that anything could happen at any time. Again, Celtic provide inspiration and drive to help me focus. I look forward to being around for the next time we play in the Champions League. I look forward to watching us lift the next trophy. I look forward to ten in a row. Sometimes I even just look as far away as the next game. That is something I need. Along with other things in my life that I can't imagine being without, these events give me motivation to be here. So I look after myself. I do as much as I can to stay as healthy as I can and I do it so that I can enjoy these moments. I know, as we all do, that someday I will enjoy my last great Celtic moment but having something inside so strong, that place that Celtic take me to, I feel more in control of when that last great moment will be.

That is where Celtic fit in to my life. I think it is pretty mind blowing that a football club can do that. The thing is, we all know Celtic are much more than just a club.

Remember just how lucky you are to be part of something as special. Remember that other fans don't have what we have. Remember you won't have it forever so please remember to cherish every moment of it.

Boavista

Daniel Cole

It was a wet Thursday night in Dumbarton. I was ten years old, in Primary six at St. Michael's Primary and it was our Easter Holidays.

Usually when nearing the end of the Easter Holidays, say the second week about Thursday/Friday, there's always a sense of 'aw naw Monday is round the corner' but not in 2003. Why? Because Celtic were locked in an intense battle in a European Semi Final with Boavista in Portugal.

I watched the first leg in Safeway at their TV section. Long story cut short: when you're a twin, even if it's a sister you have, you have to share everything, even tickets for European Semi Finals at Celtic Park.

Anyway, all thoughts of hating my sister were vanished when me and a wee skiver from his work danced in delight as Larsson squeezed in the equaliser. I was only ten but even I felt our chance was maybe gone.

But one thing you could never do was write Celtic off, especially after winning away at Blackburn and Liverpool, and of course getting an unassailable 2-0 lead early doors in Stuttgart. So maybe it was a good thing that Celtic 'hud tae come oot and go for it' in the second leg.

Fast forward a fortnight and I'm sitting in my cousin's nervously gripped to the telly as Celtic seemed to forget how to attack in Boavista. But then, with just about ten minutes left on the clock. Deliverance.

Larsson's footballing ability seemed to pass him by as he frantically swung a left foot at the ball, no technique, no composure, no power. No worries.

Ricardo dived but he was getting nowhere near it and playfully helped it on its way. By the time he looked up to see the ball in the net I was already at the bottom of a three man pile up. 'YEEEEEEEEEESSSSSSS HENRIK YA HERO HENRIK YA PURE PURE PUUUUURE BELTER YE.'

As the clock slipped away I no longer felt ten, I felt about fifty as the nerves got to me.

When Boavista charged forward 'you've got school on Monday' said my conscience. The ball harmlessly sailed over the bar and injury time was up. 'Fuck school! We're in a European Final.'

A lot can happen over the years, especially in the world of football, and where most of us struggle to remember what happened last week, we all remember vividly the moment we realised Larsson's shot had trickled in. The internet crashed that night, not because everyone was coming on Twitter to praise the manager or tweet him tactics for the final (or nude pics of yerself) but because everyone was trying to book tickets and flights for Seville.

We all know what happened in the final, but it's important to look back and remember that night in Portugal. I find myself wondering, in years to come, if I'm lucky enough to still be writing about Celtic, will I be able to talk about us reaching another European Final ? Only time will tell. But here's to you 2003, you were like a burd who'd let you walk her home before slamming the door in your face.

Fergus McCann – The Bunnet

Paul Colvin

He looked like something from the past,

People mocked but he laughed last

From Canada, back home he came

To buy our club and keep the name

The saint who wore the Bunnet, that's McCann.

He stepped in and saved our souls

Told us of his plans and goals

This modern day Messiah saved

The club we love from football's grave,

The man who wore the cap, Fergus McCann.

He read to them the riot act

As the board and manager were sacked

Then demolished our old Paradise

As we watched on with tearful eyes

But like The Lord, it rose back up again.

Fergus was a home grown fan,

Shrewd, astute, a business man

All five promises were kept

Yet some Celtic fans saw that inept

But he's the reason we still play today.

Don't underestimate his work

This solo worker never shirked

But was his just financial gain?

You decide, you've got a brain!

But what The Bunnet said, The Bunnet did!

He gave sixty thousand fans their seats

The humbled Huns could not compete

Then he saved our club from bankruptcy

And left us with his legacy,

The Paradise that we enjoy today.

He took the SFA to court

And booted Farry out the door

UEFA came next, he won that too

The Huns thought this, some kind of coup

But he done this for The Celtic that he loved.

When he returns to Celtic Park

We show respect to this class act

With all things Celtic, was obsessed

Condemning those who caused distress

A man whose heart still beats in green and white.

I think a statue should be raised

To the man whom Celtic fans should praise

Without him, no team running 'round,

We wouldn't even have a ground,

We send our deepest thanks, Fergus McCann.

Martin O'Neill Grabbed Me

Morrisey the 23rd

Heavy snow fell as we drove to Pittodrie for the 7:35pm kick-off on the Saturday the 22nd of December, 2001. We expected the game to be called off, so we listened to the radio waiting for that announcement. It never came.

Everyone found it difficult to stay on their feet in the icy conditions. The Celtic players more so. For the first time all season our players looked agitated and made clumsy errors. Chris Sutton missed a great chance from close-range when he chose the wrong foot to shoot from a beautifully delivered Stiliyan Petrov cross. Bobo Balde skied an opportunity. When the Scottish Premier League's top scorer, Henrik Larsson, fluffed a chance in the six-yard box, it felt like it was going to be one of those nights. We'd seen them before and knew it wasn't going to end well.

To take our minds off events on the park we did what everyone does in these situations; we threw snowballs at each other. Aberdeen fans took it a step further and started throwing them at Celtic players. John Hartson being a particularly popular target.

Midway through the first half Alan Thomson and Stiliyan Petrov were bombarded so badly with snowballs referee, Stuart Dougal, stopped the game. Petrov had taken a direct hit in the face so the ref asked the police to try and halt the continuous stream of missiles. By that I mean he asked the police to try and stop those in the South Stand throwing snowballs at Celtic players, not for the police to stop throwing snowballs at our players. At least I never saw any on-duty cops throwing snowballs at our players.

The inevitable arrived when Robbie Winters scored a penalty after a needless handball from Hartson. Worse followed when Darren Mackie took advantage of the latest in a series of blunders committed by November's 'player of the month', keeper Rab Douglas. Big Rab's messing up of a simple back-pass resulted in an on-form Aberdeen ending the game 2-0 winners equalling, their club record set by Alex Ferguson's side in 1983/4 of nine wins in a row.

There were nine yellow cards and a red for Aberdeen captain Derek Whyte for 'showing aggression' on this bitter night. Neil Lennon was booked on ninety minutes for dissent. After the game he sprinted into the tunnel for protection from a barrage of snowballs. Not the worst pitch-side assault he'd endured in his career.

We finished the night on 52 points, ten ahead of Rangers, with a game in-hand, even though Rangers gained points on us earlier in the day by beating Dundee United 3-2 at home. We also enjoyed a superior goal difference.

It's always a long drive home when Celtic get beat up North. The late kick-off also meant it was going to be a dark one and, as it had snowed like crazy all day, it was going to be much slower than usual. The traffic on the sludgy road continually sprayed our car's windows with dirt resulting in windscreen washers working non-stop to give us a hint of visibility. Before long we ran out of windscreen-wiper fluid and had to stop at the nearest garage to top-up. No sooner had we pulled out of the petrol station, and our driver, Joe Cassidy, had to pull into a lay-by about a mile later, just before the Perth turn-off, to wipe condensation from the inside of the window.

Having studied agriculture I stepped over the farmer's fence at the lay-by to look at the barley, and have a smoke. As I stood puffing away in the darkness the Celtic team bus pulled into the lay-by in front of Joe's car. I moved to the fence next to his car and we mouthed to each other: "That's the team bus!" We looked at each other, confused why it had also stopped in the middle-of-nowhere. A car then pulled in between Joe's car and the bus. Someone got out and went to the door of the bus. Because it was pitch black I couldn't see who so I edged closer for a better look. It was Martin O'Neill's number two, John Robertson. Just as I was thinking about whether or not to say hello to John our manager Martin O'Neil stepped down from the bus and they had a quick chat. Apart from the parked car there wasn't any reason for them to suspect anyone else was nearby. I felt like a snooper but didn't know if I should interrupt them and let them know I was there. Before I had time to decide Martin took the car keys and John boarded the bus, which closed its doors and pulled away.

As Martin made his way towards the car I shouted, "Martin O'Neill! You're a legend!"

He peered through the driving snow and saw me wearing long-sleeved hoops and smoking a fag.

"You still think that after today's performance?" he asked.

"It's Christmas and that's the first points we've dropped all season. We're going to win the league!" I announced while stepping back over the fence.

I stubbed my cigarette out. He opened the car's back door and threw his suit jacket onto the seat. He then slammed the door shut and briskly marched towards me. Even in the poor conditions I could see he looked mad. I braced myself to receive pelters from Martin O'Neill.

My feet slipped on the slush and my arms flailed to right myself as Martin grabbed my Celtic shirt by the scruff of the neck. I scrambled to get away. Not because I was scared. Not because...but because it was Martin O'Neil. Normally, if someone tried to grab me I'd make sure I hit them first. But how could I possibly hit him back even if he hit me first? Imagine being known as the fan who punched Martin O'Neill? Even my brothers would hunt me down.

The back lights of the Celtic bus glowed in the distance. Windscreen wipers beat time in Joe's car as his splodged turnip face rubbed half-moons on the passenger window and gawked out. He'd have probably ended up giving Martin handers anyway.

Martin held tight and looked right into my eyes, smiled and said in a very determined Northern Ireland burr: "You better believe it!"

I think we then exchanged pleasantries. I don't remember. I was still in shock at Martin O'Neill being so close to me I could see the halo of his breath.

He got into his car and drove away.

I watched him disappear into the night before climbing into Joe's car. "What did he say to you?"

I told him and he burst out laughing. Suddenly we didn't care about the snow, the poor performance or the slow drive home. We guessed that they had arranged to meet there so the bus could go to Glasgow and Martin O'Neill could take the Edinburgh road home.

Strangely enough, the previous season we stopped to refuel at a petrol station on the way back from Aberdeen and the team bus pulled in there. The same switcheroo happened with John Robertson and Martin O'Neil, except many other Celtic supporters who'd also stopped for petrol mobbed Martin from the bus to his car. They must have decided to avoid similar scenes by stopping in a remote, peaceful place.

I phoned one of my brothers who lived in Germany and was known to users of Celtic Quick News as 'Awe Naw No Annoni On Anaw Noo'. "Were gonnae win the league!" I told him.

"Oh Aye? What makes you think that?"

"I just met Martin O'Neill and he told me."

When we got home we watched the highlights recorded on BBC. In the post-match interview Chic Young asked Martin something along the lines of, 'Do you still think you can win the league?' to which Martin replied something along the lines of, 'Well, there's still a long way to go... Rangers are the benchmark...'

I shouted at the telly, "Grab him by the throat like you did with me and tell him what you told me."

This game was to be the only league game we lost that season. For sweet revenge we beat Aberdeen away on the last game of the season and also finished eighteen points ahead of our benchmark. Martin O'Neill was too busy celebrating to meet up with me. I didn't hold it against him.

Asperger, Internet and Celtic

Joshua Gaffney

I was four years old when diagnosed with Asperger syndrome. I also had a stutter throughout primary school. Football never interested me. I was a very logical kid. I viewed it as men just kicking a ball around a field. Sometimes kids in the playground wanted to talk to me about football. All I knew was my dad and his family supported Celtic. I picked them as my team, even though I'd never watched them. This decision didn't really help me as there was only one other Celtic fan in the school around my age. Everyone else was a Rangers fan. When I reached primary six, a few weeks in, Celtic beat Rangers 6-2, and this kick-started my interest in football. But I could only watch Celtic games on BBC or STV. On my way to school I popped into a corner shop and got a Freddo bar or two. This gave me an excuse to have a peak at the back pages of the papers. The person at the till never bothered.

Several years passed and I was about to move into third year of academy, but my family had to move to a new town and that meant a different school. This is usually a big social challenge to any teenager, but for someone with Asperger it's a nightmare.

At the new school I wasn't socially terrible, but I interacted less well than in my old academy. Outside school I found a few friends nearby and, for the first time in my life, was able to play football (mostly mini-games). However, the biggest step I took to becoming a fully-fledged Celtic fan was when I got my first computer (Dell Dimension 4600) along with fibre-optic internet. I'd used the internet before, but having my own personal computer in my bedroom opened up many possibilities.

In 2005 Celtic were a few weeks into their season under Gordon Strachan. I'd watched our 5-0 defeat at the hands of Artmedia Bratislava while on holiday in Gran Canaria and thought "fucking great". The season got worse when we lost 3-1 to Rangers, but I was still hopeful. It was the first time in my life we had a Celtic kit that I really liked, and I could watch all of the games thanks to our Telewest box and get all the gossip on the internet.

It wasn't long until I stumbled upon a Celtic forum, (talkceltic.net). This opened up a whole new method of communication for me. As someone with Asperger I struggled with face-to-face social interaction. On the internet, however, it's just text, so I was treated truly as an equal. With the help of one of my friends I learned how to get the most out of my computer. I loved one program in particular: Macromedia Fireworks MX. It allowed me to be a bit of an artist. I'd always liked art but could never master drawing or painting. I combined my fledgling programming skills with the Celtic forum to achieve some sort of social responsibility. My job was to create avatars and signatures for other Celtic fans. I created graphics for the forum itself and was promoted to a moderator because my work was so good. Even though this isn't the type of accomplishment that will feature in a Hollywood blockbuster, or win you the Nobel prize, it was important to me. In real life I was shy, socially awkward and never really got into the action, but on the internet I was in there. I was involved. I felt like I was a part of something.

In 2007 I created my own forum with the help of my Rangers-supporting friend. He picked the name, celtictalk.org. The name caused some problems, but that wasn't important. My aim was to have more freedom so my skills, and the skills of others, could help create the best forum. It never grew to the size of other Celtic forums, but I did not create it to become the most popular forum, just the best for me and whoever used it. During this time I learned a valuable lesson. With more freedom comes more responsibility. I had to deal with personal, political and racial conflicts, which have been tough, but I learned valuable lessons.

I've grown older and gained, and I've sought to bridge the gap between the freedom of the internet and real life. I turned twenty-one and stumbled across a writer named Paul Larkin who wrote about Celtic. I've never been into books and had never heard of this guy before, but I promoted him on my site because he looked the real deal to Celtic fans who liked books. A few months later I got my first invite to a Celtic event: Paul's first book launch in Scotland.

I started to use Twitter quite often and got involved in what is now Hail Hail Media. This brought me into contact with a lot more Celtic fans who did stuff with Celtic on and off the internet-- exactly what I was looking for.

The book launch couldn't have went any better. That day we beat Kilmarnock 6-0 to win the league. Guinness flowed and songs were sung. This is something I want to do again. The Celtic family and the internet helped me deal with my Asperger, and that is why Celtic is more than a football club.

Moonlight Over Paradise

John C Traynor

Moonlight over Paradise

took his breath away -

he'd never seen the old place look that way.

He'd stepped out for a breath of air

at the end of a long, hard day...

that moonlight stirred the ghost of history

in Celtic Park.

Young Lennon was an Irish Tim -

a flame-haired Lurgan Bhoy.

He burned with love of Celtic ...

sure, they were his pride and joy.

With a dream to thrill the faithful

from Hong Kong to Illinois,

he set off along the road to Paradise!

His promise blossomed early,

took him o'er the Irish sea -

but something drew him homeward

to re-think his destiny.

Re-focused, he was ready,

he was off and running free

down the long and winding road to Paradise!

Moonlight over Paradise

took his breath away -

he'd never seen the old place look that way.

He'd stepped out for a breath of air

at the end of a long, hard day...

that moonlight cast a cloak of mystery

on Celtic Park.

When his mentor came a-calling

in that soft, persuasive voice,

O'Neill was on the march

and Lenny really had no choice.

Consistency, composure,

growing stature, power and poise

took him further down the road to Paradise!

Then, as fate unfolded,

came the call from Celtic Park.

The hour had come for Lenny ...

it was time to make his mark;

to play a Captain's role,

of dwindling Hope to be the spark -

he had finally found his way to Paradise!

Moonlight over Paradise

took his breath away -

he'd never seen the old place look that way.

He'd stepped out for a breath of air

at the end of a long, hard day ...

that moonlight augured Lenny's destiny

at Celtic Park.

The Day We Stopped The Ten

Wullie Broon

What am I doin' in a tent? The hazy mist of my hangover shifts to the right and my heid whacks the canvas as I struggle up into something resembling perpendicular. There's the soles of a pair of sannies aboot three feet away. It's my brother. He's neether inside nor ootside the tent. No doubt he just slept where he fell. Still can't remember why we're in a tent. I turn roon. Ma wee lassie and ma nephew are also oot for the count, but they're in sleeping bags. That's right, we're campin' oot in ma brother's garden.

I lie back doon to try and get back to sleep but it hits me and I jump up, heid whacking the canvas so hard I nearly wake the weans. My stomach's convulsing and my heart's racing like a Scaletrix with fresh batteries. It's bad enough the Huns bought their way to equal our nine, but we cannae let them beat it. We need to win the league today and stop this ten-in-a-row shite.

The sun begins to sweat the inside of the tent and something doesn't smell too healthy. Think it might be me. My heid's nippin' but I find two Co-proximol in ma back pocket which, although no as good as being drunk, is no a bad way to start the day.

I gie the wean a shunt. "Mon, it's time to go hame, it's big party day." We climb over ma brother and head hame in a hurry, but when we get in the hoose I find oot it's only 6.20am. I go to my bed and try again to sleep but it's no happenin'. I end up sitting like a sack of totties on the couch waitin' for Soccer AM to come oan.

It's 10.30am before ma brother Kenny phones. Not only has he managed to recover, he's even been to the toon and back, and he's goin' mental. "We need to go doon the Garngad. Wait till ye see it, I'll be roon wi' the motor in ten minutes."

I've been doin' the gas servicing for a couple of the local housing associations in the Garngad and got to know everybody and their dugs. It's a great place, full of Tims and fine people. I was working doon there yesterday wi ma apprentice, wee Rab. We kept looking oot the window, when we should have been workin', and smilin' at each other because the bunting was starting to go up.

Today I'm wearing a new Celtic top. I'm thinking new top new era. I've also got on my lucky Nike baseball boots. We've never lost when I've worn them. Hang on a minute. Have we won every game, or have we just no' been beaten? This becomes the most important question in the universe. We need to win today—a draw's no use. I sit up straight and put the thinking heid oan. I wore the Nikes when we won the League Cup against Dundee United. But what about when Lambert scored that screamer against the Huns at New Year? Did we win that game or draw it? It takes me while but I get there and smile, which is never a pretty sight, but aye, we won that 2-0. Sorted.

Eventually Kenny turns up wi the car and I jump in. When we turn into Royston Road I'm in awe. It's covered green and white wi flags, bunting, scarves and dugs wi Celtic tops on. We take a ride up 'the hill' and the whole place looks amazing.

The O'Brian's have a huge CSC banner drapped oot their windaes. We're totally buzzing and start rocking the car, blasting out the Celtic songs. Time for a carry oot.

An auld man shouts across the street, "Good luck tae yer team the day, son!" and he disnae even look drunk.

I gie him a big smile and thumbs up before heading intae the off sales. The guys running it, Shahid and Ricky, are good Tims. They're buzzing and have decided Saturday is a hauf- day for them so they can go to the game. I shout up my usual dozen cans and bottle of wine and as I leave their shop we aw shake hands.

Fully loaded we hurry back to ma hoose for a swally. Once that first can is sparked I start thinking aboot decorating the living room for the after-match party. Then I gie myself a row for thinking too far ahead. Whit if something goes wrong, or what if Henrik has an aff day, which is much the same thing?

I take a deep swallow of Tennents and pour myself a wee Buckie to shake aff negativity. Charged up, I jump oot the chair and race upstairs to find the two big framed collages I've made from cutting from this season's Celtic Views. I've one for the League Cup win, complete with a cup-final ticket, and one, set aside, for winning the League (I'm praying) complete wi the stub you get in yer season book. I tack both of them up oan the Analglypta in the living room. Then I gargle a quick swallow of Tennents to help my eyesight and stick all the Celtic players' pics on the wall beside them. There's not enough wall space and I need tae stick some up in the hall. The final touch is my six 'Celtic- Beer' bottles with candles in them on the mantelpiece. The living room is a shrine to good taste and decency.

We park doon at the Forge on the Gallowgate for a quick getaway after the game. I have a few cans whilst sitting in the car, before we join the throng walking roon to Celtic Park. The police are out wae their horses. Kenny and me fall into a steady step and start chin-wagging and reminiscing. It's mobbed and there's no space on the pavement between us, but that doesn't matter, it's always been Kenny and me at the fitbaw. Our Granda used to take us to see Partick Thistle. Then we got hooked on the hard-stuff, going on the Springburn bus to see Celtic in the 70's-- right up to the present season. We're brothers, Celtic supporters and best mates.

Even with a drink the nerves have taken over. My mouth's going 100 mph and his hits 110 mph. We cannae believe it's been ten years since Andy Walker rattled in the third goal against Dundee at the old Celtic Park to win the league in our Centenary year, and that ten years have passed before we might be champions again. Kenny said something about that's how our uncles must have felt before Lisbon in '67.

We reach our seats high up in section 417, excitedly gibbering away wi all the new pals we've made since the new stadium opened. Everybody is the same, nerves like newly strung banjo wire, but trying to kid oan we're all confident that beating St Johnstone and winning the league will be easy.

The teams come out and the noise nearly knocks us down. Not that we're supposed to be standing, of course.

I scream at the top of my voice, "C'mon the hoops!" over and over again. It's the adrenalin. It's nerves. It's God help us win. I'm thinking what the noise will be like when the new Celtic end of the ground is completed. The game kicks off. Everyone is on their feet singing constantly. What would I give for an early goal today? Most fans in the stadium, I believe, would consider sacrificing their soul to the devil for all of eternity, as long as the devil's not a Proddy, to ensure the result goes our way today.

A throw-in from the left. Henrik picks up the ball and goes on a mazy run towards the box. He's about twenty yards out. He's walloped it. "Yes! Ya fuckin' dancer!"

The place is going mental. *'We shall not; we shall not be moved not by the Hearts, the Hibs or the Rangers; we shall not be moved!'*

We can smell the title. It's in our grasp. I sit down wishing there wasn't another 84 minutes to go.

Despite good possession we're still waiting for that killer second goal. It's a mad feeling because technically, at this point, we are the champions, but one goal from St Johnstone can destroy everything. Everybody knows that, but nobody wants to jinx it by saying anything.

The second half starts. I look down and realise I've been sitting rubbing ma hauns up and doon ma thighs like some lunatic. I'm almost sure I never asked ma hauns to dae that, but that's wit they're daein. I'm a mess. Only one thing outside St Johnstone scoring can make me feel worse. Then it happens. Harald Brattbakk comes on as a sub for Simon Donnelly.

I'm no saying he'll no score today, or he's shite - he'd a good scoring record before we signed him - but he's probably goin to miss aboot ten sitters.

I'm cracking up, shouting and swearing at the Hun ref. Harald takes about five minutes before he touches the ball. His control is never that good.

Cannae stop clock-watching; every minute feels like an hour. It's murder. I'm murder. St Johnstone are killing me. That wee Hun bastard George O'Boyle's had a couple of good chances. Thank God he duffed them. I'm sweating and swearing like a Proddy. I want Celtic to score, or I want to black oot and wake up when the game's done. I'd leave if I could, but I cannae. I might even go for a walk to calm doon.

Tommy Boyd's got the ball in the corner, just below us. He bombs up the wing, but there's a guy zoomin' in on him. I'm up screamin', trying to warn Boyd: "Stop fuckin' aboot Boyd! Get the baw tae fuck up the park!"

A guy jumps up in front of me, so Ah need to a bend ma heid roond just in time to see the baw shooting across the penalty box. There's Harrald, BANG!

"Yes! Goalll!"

Pressure and tension evaporate, and an amazing feeling of unbridled relief, piggy-backing on joy, fills every part of my body: ma hearing goes funny, and ma heid is dizzy as a Sunday night disco, but I don't care. We're all jumping aboot hugging, kissing. I'm greeting and I'm not the only one. "We've done it!" My voice has found home. "We've fuckin' done it! We've fuckin' done it!"

This is heaven and the angels in green-and-white rise up and chant, in one voice: *"Cheerio tae yer 10 in a row!"*

The stadium vibrates with the noise and the stamping of people's feet. There's so many different songs being sung aroon the stadium that it's a colourful curtain of noise. Whistling starts in the Jock Stein stand, rises up, and takes hold of us, makes us staun on the tips of our toes, bent over, waiting. "C'moan ref blaw yer whistle!"

The ref gives a free kick, but time slows as he walks over, picks the ball up, and blows for full time. Sixty thousand supporters jump into the air. The foundations of the newly-built stadium hold firm. We've done it. We Are The Champions.

We celebrate Tommy Boyd lifting the trophy as if he's given birth to it. It's a wonderful feeling. The team are doing the lap of honour in their 'Smell The Glove' tee-shirts. I canny take my eyes off that trophy. Our trophy. That beautiful piece of silverware. That's what it's all about. The fans and players have paid a blood toll for the sheer arrogance of that mob from Govan who thought they could buy their way to the record books. Our club almost died, despite, the beautiful, yet unsuccessful, football of the Tommy Burns era. The Hun bubble is now well and truly burst.

On the way back from the stadium I get Kenny to stop at an off-sales we know on Carntyne road. I fire in through the door and the wee guy who runs the shop is over the moon. He's tells me his son has been phoning from their home town in India all day getting updates on the score. I pick up a bottle of Buckfast and put it on the counter. "How much?"

"For you, my friend, only £2."

"That's nearly as good as the result," I say, giving him a big pat on the back.

We take a detour along Royston Road and the place is heaving. I'm riding shotgun, standing up through the sunroof, shouting and waving to everybody.

We're just passing the Big Glen when someone shouts, "There's the big gas man!"

We get the wives, dump the car and head back doon.

We arrive, large cargo in hand, for the best street-party in the world-- EVER! Our family and mates are all there. Supporters buses begin taking detours through Royston Road on their way home, adding to the magical feeling of camaraderie. This is us. This is the Celtic Family. It's like buzzing on E's except you love everybody multiplied by ten. There's a band playing. I'm sure it's Charlie and the Bhoys, but there's so many people we canny get near them.

We make our own solution and climb up the scaffolding on to the tenement roof. It's a perfect spot for a liquid picnic. Fae up here we can hear and see the band and watch the huge party of jubilant Tims below.

It's not long before we're joined by a few others, then a few more, and then many more. It's no tickets and standing room only, but we manage to get a good bit of craic before Strathclyde's finest ask us to remove ourselves, or they'll help spoil the party.

When we finally get back to oor hoose the place is jumping. There's ma family, extended family, the Keenan's, the Forrest's and Scoobie O'Hara. A finer bunch of unrepentant Fenians you'll never meet. The weans are aw oot running up and doon the street wi their brand new 'Champions 98' flags, absolutely loving it. All the grown-ups are indoors, partying away to Celtic songs. I've not seen everyone buzzing like this for a long time, but I've a feeling there will be more nights like this to come. The Celtic faith inside me is bubbling up, telling me we've come through the worst, and climbed back to the top, without ever losing our dignity.

That's the Celtic way.

The Exiles' Dream

John C Traynor

Exiles' dream, grand old team, Glasgow Celtic,

bridging the past and today –

Celtic! ... Celtic! ... Celtic!,

we'll be with you every step of the way.

It began as the dream of our fathers.

Brother Walfrid inspired them to play.

It still burns in the hearts of the faithful –

dear old Celtic, we'll be with you all the way ...

... joyfully sharing the good times -

proud to stand firm through the bad ...

... sav'ring each sweet taste of glory -

and bearing what heartache we've had.

We were there at the start in our fathers -

they live on in our spirit today.

In the hearts of our own sons and daughters,

we'll stay with you every step of the way ...

... living that dream of our fathers -

true to their hopes we have been ...

... playing our part in the story -

wrapped in the hoops, white and green.

Weaned on great stories

of Quinn and McGrory

and Tully, the jester supreme;

thrill after thrill

on the road to Seville,

as we marched with O'Neill

and a dream.

Legends like Maley,

Dan Doyle, Jim Delaney,

bold Patsy, the Lions and Stein;

Larsson was "King of Kings".

Aye! ... but wee Jinky's

the greatest Celt

there's ever been!

... glad of our place in the story,

we become part of the dream ...

... steeped in the songs and the legend ...

true to our roots and our genes.

Like the hopes and the dreams of our fathers,

evergreen the tradition will stay,

with the Hoops linking all generations -

all together, all for Celtic, all the way ...

... we'll be with you, every step of the way ...

... Glasgow Celtic, we'll be with you, all the way!

The Celtic Spirit

Pat Marrinan

The lounge in Terminal One at the world's busiest airport, Heathrow, never sleeps, but at night it slows to a walk after a day of frenetic activity.

One of the airport staff met Cal and guided him to the lounge. A nice young woman with sympathetic voice and slight Asian accent said she'd return for him when it was time to board the flight. The Glasgow flight was delayed and Cal knew he'd have at least two hours to kill before heading home. He thanked her and listened as the click click click of her high heels grew fainter.

Cal put his bag and cane down and sat in a quiet seat by the big picture window. Chill November sunshine had given way to darkness and cold rains ran down the glass like a million tears. The runway's hypnotic lights sparkled like gems, and beyond them the lights of the London skyline flickered.

But having lost his sight in an industrial accident years earlier Cal was oblivious. At first he struggled learning to use other senses to navigate the world but wasn't one for giving up. His hearing became especially sharp as he used it more to compensate for his loss of sight.

'Is this seat taken, son?' a gruff Scottish voice inquired, stirring Cal from his thoughts.

'Naw, sit down pal,' Cal answered in his usual Glaswegian accent.

'Ankle's sore again,' the man went on. 'Old injury from my playing days.'

Cal smiled at the familiar tone of the stranger but couldn't quite place him. 'Ye a footballer or a rugby man?'

'I was a footballer, nothing special, son, long time ago, but sometimes the old injuries still give me a bit of pain. But it's a minor thing really.'

Cal enjoyed chatting to other commuters on his many travels and refused to become a recluse just because he'd lost his sight. He knew some weren't comfortable talking to a blind man but tonight felt reassured by the stranger's voice. 'Heading hame?'

'Aye. Heading home right enough. What about you?'

'I'm going tae the Celtic Barcelona match tomorrow night.' Cal knew from experience that conversations either warmed or cooled once he declared himself as a Celt. On this occasion it warmed.

'Should be a great game,' the man said. 'I recall a lot of great teams going down at Celtic Park. Best atmosphere in Europe on those big nights under the lights.'

Despite the fact he couldn't see him Cal turned to face the man. 'Do ye think Celtic have any chance? I mean Barcelona are some outfit these days.'

'Listen, son, I saw Jimmy Johnstone destroy Red Star Belgrade in half an hour at Celtic Park. I saw Leeds, the invincible Leeds, go down at Hampden. Anything is possible in football, especially where Celtic and that support are involved. You just need enough belief and enough talent.'

Cal laughed. 'I love yer optimism; I just wish I shared it. We could get battered by Barca tomorrow.'

'Ach, son, this is Celtic we're talking about. They raise it on these nights. Lenny will get them motivated and organised.'

They talked for over an hour reliving great European nights from the distant past as well as more recent history.

Cal said, 'O'Neill's team gave us some great nights. Beating Liverpool was classic. Celtic were total underdogs and beat them in their own stadium, too.'

'You know your stuff, son.' He laughed. 'I can see you're a real Celtic man.'

'Learned it all at ma Da's knee. He was a great Celtic man and passed it on tae me.'

The man adopted a more sombre tone. 'Is your Da still alive, son?'

Cal's smile faded. 'Naw, lost him a few years back. He was a miner. Lungs were ruined in the pits.'

'Aye...ruined a lot of good man that industry. A dark and dangerous place to make a living. But it forged strong bonds, too. You had to depend on each other down there.' He stopped for a second before continuing, 'Do you mind telling me how you lost your sight, son?'

Cal liked his straightforwardness and replied in an equally matter of fact voice, 'I worked in the petro-chemical industry and some sloppy work and stupid cost-cutting led to a chemical leak. Stupid really. I thought I could sort it without wearing the oxygen suit. I was wrong. A cloud of mixed gases, mostly phosgene and hydrogen cyanide built up, took my sight, lucky to survive it really.'

'And you're travelling on your own to see Celtic? That takes some bottle, son. Good on you.'

'I'm no one for lying down tae these things. My Da taught me that. Not the Celtic way, giving up, is it?'

'Ach yer a true Celt right enough. I'll need to go now, son, but here's something for you.' He pressed what felt like an envelope into Cal's hand.

'Yer Da would be proud of ye.' Just as Cal was about to respond the kindly girl with the light Asian accent cut across him,

'Your flight is boarding in 20 minutes, sir. Would you like a coffee while you wait?'

'Tea would be lovely. Can ma friend have one, too?'

The girl sounded hesitant. 'Friend? There's no one here, sir. You're the only person in the lounge.'

'Are you sure? I've been talking tae a man for the last hour.'

'I've been at the desk over there all night, sir. No one has been sitting by you. Perhaps you nodded off and dreamed it?'

Cal said nothing, his hand pressing his jacket to feel for the envelope the man gave him. It was there. He hadn't dreamt it.

The following evening Cal sat in Celtic Park beside his brother in the huge North Stand. The stadium rocked as the sell-out crowd awaited the arrival of the teams. His brother described the scene to him in detail as he had done for every game Cal attended since he lost his sight.

The chill November air caressed Cal's face as he pondered Celtic's chances. What would this vibrant night offer Celtic's legions of fans? Surely they couldn't topple this great Barcelona team, could they? This was Celtic, anything is possible.

'Ten minutes to kick off, Cal, the place is packed, the big Champions League logo is covering the Centre-circle' Sean half-shouted above the noise of the crowd, helping Cal build a mental picture of the scene.

Cal shared the excitement in his brother's voice. Tonight was going to be a special night. 'Do me a favour, Sean, will ye?' He fished an envelope from his pocket. 'Could you open this and tell me what it is?'

He handed the envelope to his brother and listened as Sean tore it open.

After a moment Sean said to him, 'Where did you get this, Cal?'

'Why? What is it Sean?'

'It's a picture, Cal, an old style black and white photograph.'

Cal pushed his brother for more information. 'A picture of what?'

Sean hesitated. 'It's our Da when he was young. He's in his mining gear and his face is dirty with coal dust but I would recognise him no problem.'

Cal was stunned. 'Anything else?'

'Aye, he's standing beside another miner who looks like...well he looks like a young Jock Stein!'

The picture was passed among the fans sitting around the brothers. One old man, with grey hair protruding from his bunnet, put his glasses on and carefully studied the photo. 'Aye,' that's Jock all right. He was a miner before he became a professional player.'

Cal felt bewildered but a huge roar announced Celtic and Barcelona were coming down the tunnel. Sean described the scene as tens of thousands of coloured sheets were held up to create a stunning mosaic to celebrate Celtic's 125 years in football.

The game got underway amid a crescendo of noise with Sean describing Barcelona's probing play as they flicked the ball around with practiced ease. 'They're looking good, Cal, but no penetration at the moment.'

Cal's mind wandered back to the airport, the man and the photo. He tried to remember his voice. Did he know him? Why did he ask after his da?

'Corner to Celtic, Mulgrew is trotting over to take it,' said Sean. As the cross swung over he grabbed Cal just as Wanyama bulleted his header into the Barcelona net.

The place erupted.

'Yeeeeesss!' roared Sean, hugging Cal.

Cal celebrated with as much passion as the rest. As he jumped out his seat he lost his footing and stumbled forward. Strong and willing hands held him upright and stopped him falling into the people in front.

A voice shouted through the uproar of the goal celebration, 'Steady, son, you've got enough to contend with without breaking your neck, too!'

It was the voice from the airport. Cal knew it in an instant. Before he could ask the questions he wanted answered the man released his grip. 'Enjoy the game, son, and never doubt the Celtic spirit.'

Cal mumbled amid the raucous noise, 'I never would, not once.'

'Good', the voice said. 'Your Da would be proud of you.'

Sean grabbed Cal. 'Who are ye talking to, Cal?'

'No one, Sean.' Cal hugged his brother. 'Let's win this thing. Let's see how the mighty Barca stand up tae the Celtic Spirit!'

John Thomson

Paul Colvin

Farewell The Prince of Goalies

So tragic, such a loss

At 22, you lie there

'Neath the old stone Celtic cross.

I never got to see you

But stories, I've been told

Of the bhoy who was a legend

When you kept the Celtic goal.

Thousands walked to mourn you

But millions saw you play

And even now we speak of

The Prince who showed the way

For future Celtic 'keepers

Who stand between those posts

But a friend stands there beside them,

Young John Thomson's ghost.

I stand here by your graveside

But no tears come to my eyes

For I know that you're still living

'Tween the posts in Paradise.

Farewell, farewell young Johnny

Your story will be told

How the bhoy from Cardenden became

The Prince in Celtic's goal.

Oor Ain Wee Corner

Lorenzo Wordsmith

Years ago we vented our upsets, our frustrations and our loss of innocence down by the street corner.

We always complained vociferously when told to 'move on sonny or else' time and again, by the Polis, otherwise known as the fuzz, the rozzers, the auld bill, the coppers or the Cruelty to mention but a few of the corner warning nicknames.

In they days, they, 'the polis' didnay mind gist geen yay a 'belt in the mooth' tay perk yer ideas up. It was par for the course for the corner crew and what we expected and, tay be honest, needed at times.

Well, who wur yay gonnay complain tay anyhow? Yer ma or da?

Nay chance. They'd have leathered yay as well for bein stupid enough tay get rumbled doin whatever you shouldn't be doin.

Naybody ran tay their local MP or Human Rights orgs either. They were just faceless and spineless words that didn't meet many minds in the closes, the wee mans pubs or street corners up n doon the land. Everybody gist sucked shit up as part of normal life. We was awe in the same boat.

But hey, wur we fkn bored, man.

Oor usual explanations for the gatherings would be, 'But mister...there's bugger all to do,' or 'this harassment is a fuckin anti-teenage agenda, it's cos wur yung int it!'

What we didn't realise, no come to think of it, we didn't care about, was what a noisy destructive bunch we surely were as we kicked baws off the walls of somebody's hoose day and night.

We awe wanted tay score the winner in the European Cup Final against Inter, played oot in an auld drying green.

The constant thuddin must have drove the inhabitants nuts, no tay mention the occasional winday smash. It took the best part of a year tay get the putty guy oot, n then we'd remove the putty out of curiosity and become Tony Hart creatives for a few hours.

Aye, we was fkn pests to be sure, but we didn't care, it was training.

We was potential soccer superstars or top athletes with awe the runnin we did when the panda car appeared, top speed about 40 miles an hour. I'm sure it must have felt the same on almost every street corner across the cities of the time.

The perception's probably the same with the gangs of drink and drug-fuelled needs grouped together, hell bent on wanton destruction and being as big a nuisance as possible, or so we were often accused, which we resented, cos oor maws wid have killed us if she fun oot.

Angel-faced altar bhoys on Sunday makin yer mammy ever so proud, roving destroyers of forward progression the rest of the time. Rebels indeed, mostly without a clue.

You see, to us it was offered when challenged, as just youthful exuberance.

We got booked or apprehended for our cheek with many wide-ranging excuses. The favourite, though, in yer best innocent face, was always youthful high jinks, but that was no get out clause.

For a few adults, a few mind, it was indeed that youthful tendency they themselves had displayed but now ignored in later life, perhaps with new-found authoritative position.

He might have been a Janny or summit.

With age came responsibility you see, until yer auld man was as pished as a fart, then it was 'who fuckin cares aboot awe that shite man. Leave the lads alone, you forget when you were a kid, pal!'

That was a common statement from the blind-with-rage parent, usually though, from the parent who's kids could do no wrong, ever.

You know the ones I mean, it still goes on.

'Naw pal, no ma boy, he widnay day that, noo fuck off afore a get pissed off n put yer lights oot!'

'Hey man, it's only some graffiti, a wee bit of spray paint, a coupla menshees, the kids is bored shitless.'

'It's only some broken bottles and fag ends, fuck sake, it happens awe the time err a gathering of underage drinkers on their journey to manhood, don't it, geeza break ya nosey fud.'

The rank smell of pish from the corner of the walls or shop shutters was normal, 'so wit, it's natural int it?'

'Wit you want, dude, the kids tay pish thur bloody pants!'

Inside oor wee heads, as we listened to the adult back-up bicker way the moaner, we was thinking, 'Nah fuck you Mr Doogood, it's oor scheme, oor street, oor fuckin corner, noo bolt ya dafty!'

All the squabbling, screaming and fighting of a weekend night was par for the course, man. It was gangland kinda shit wint it? Besides, being outside of that, on them mean streets was fatal man.

There wisnay many hapless victims in ma hood.

Mibee somebody finished the last sip a cider or vino, or somebody got twos up oan the last Capstan full strength or Woodbine throat choker nicked oot somebody's granda's tin without even declaring an interest in a smoke until that mornin.

But that was no reason for any of the senior citizens or educated proper folk way the best togs, nay mates and proper speak, tay fear poppin oot for a loaf, a bag a sugar or a newspaper, was it?

The street corner was as safe as hooses, man, gist get some baws and get yer shoppin in ya dumplin.

Aye, them days was no half educational.

Mibee no the educationals we needed, but they did teach us shit never the less. We learned how tay act big, be the toughest of the softest and curse in a variety of tongues.

'No wit a meen, ya wanker.'

As we started to expand our horizons at the weekends, the majority of us fae the same school and same school of thought, would get a right few of us together and head tay Parkheed for the game, done up in awe wur greenery.

It was the birth right you see, the real religious festival.

This deprived deluge of kids from the corners of destruction knew how to express their beliefs, we had voices and we was gonna use them, we believed in Celtic, we still do.

'Hail Hail the Celts are here...and off we'd go, sun's oot, troops are sorted, who geez a fuck.'

'The hills are alive way the sound of...sa bastard.' 'For it's a Grand old team to....' the sounds belted oot.

Naybody gave a toss. The modern day 'kettle' hudnay been invented yet and the hospital casualty was a natural result of the acceptable chaos.

In they days, you could stand, sing, move, smoke, eat and drink, piss ootside and it wiz seen as normal.

This was pre-political correctness in the days when the law was catchin criminals not creating them.

Sure, to us that other lot in blue was worse than we could ever be. We awe ran the gauntlet of the fitba day oot, and loved it.

Back then real freedom wisnay a crime you see.

We could express, depress and produce the middle fingers with ease. The street corner had made us professionals at it.

We'd chip wur coins the gether, manage a couple tins of the ale, fags, wur fare for the rockin bus as pensioners covered their ears and hoped we would get aff next stop as we planned our way intay the sacred grun.

'Here goes for the punty err, try n make yerself look smaller it usually worked a treat, man.'

Some of the guys dane the liftin err - good guys that remembered their street corners - some of them still livin there to this day having moved from the Eldee tay the Buckie, near keeled err hauf the time liftin err these young looking adults and questioned 'wit fkn age ur you pal?' usually tay the back of yer heed as you squeezed yer torso intay the grun and legged it to a rendezvous point.

'Fanks mister Jimmy!'

'Hail Hail' and off, past the stampede of other successful punties to catch up way who else goat in fae yer ain crew.

'For we will be mastered by no..... Lively crowd the day lads..!' 'Geeza fag man eh, am gaspin.'

'Hail Hail the Celts are here...' and off we'd go, who gives a fuck, we're in paradise.

Years of that went on, man. Doggin school tay sneak a peek at the weekend's upcoming project, who we playin next, where aboots, how do we get there?

We started properly shavin, gettin laid, gettin educated about the real meanin of Celtic, real priorities, we was get'n awe political and managin tay still make sure the street corner we held firm at the games remained the same.

'Fuck the suits, man,' cos sure as fuck, they was fuckin us. Aye, the street corner was an education. It 'husnay hauf' expanded.

Yon Night

Tom Leonard

yonwuz sum night

thi Leeds gemmit Hamdin

a hunnirn thurty four thousan

aw singin

yilnivir wok alone

wee burdnma wurk then

nutsnur a wuz

but she wuzny intristid

yi no thi wey

well there wuzza stonnin

ana wuz thaht happy

ana wuz thaht fed up

hoffa mi wuz greetnaboot Celtic

anhoffa mi wuz greetnaboot hur

big wain thata wuz

a kin laffitit noo

Big Jock Stein and Me

Jack O'Donnell

Mum asked me to babysit Granda. He was going a bit doowally. I didn't really think it was fair. It was her dad. Not mine. But I knew one thing that got him going, more than a half and half-pint, was talking about fitba. I let him settle into his chair, close enough for him to shout at the telly and hit it with his walking-stick when changing channels, before I even mentioned Celtic.

"Aye, Jock Stein won the European Cup in 1967," said Granda and that was him off and running, and he didn't even need a ball.

"Everybody was always going on about how great it was that a team made up of players from twelve square miles of Glasgow had won the European Cup. But the truth is, even the Huns got to a European final that year."

Granda gave me a minute to digest this and clack his falsers. I gawked out the living-room window of his sheltered-housing complex, wondering when I could escape to the rich grass of Singer's Park that ran like an extended back garden for dogs to shit on outside, whilst arranging my face to be suitably amazed.

"And they were Protestants."

"Really," I said. "The Huns, were Protestants!"

"Yes," said Granda, searching my face for signs of dissent, but I wasn't arguing, not today.

"Yes," Granda said, "Protestants and you know that not one Protestant would ever have got near the Celtic team, but that team that one the European Cup weren't even as good as the team from The View."

"Twelve square miles," said Granda, more and more clacking spittle spraying out with each word. He was getting worked up again. "The team from the View. Two square miles. That was a team. That was a team that would have won the European cup."

Granda handed me the framed photo of him and Jimmy Johnstone again. Jimmy had his arm around Granda's shoulder and they were both posing for the camera, in the almost mandatory bare-legged, half-kneeling, half-sitting stance. They were almost identical, with their cropped curly hair, a ball at their feet and smiles so broad they suggested the sun would never stop shining. Granda looked younger than me.

"Jock Stein. Jock Stein. He'd won the Scottish Cup with Dunfermline and he'd been captain of Celtic. People said he was a miner. But he wasnae a miner. He was a bastard and worse than that he was a Protestant. Everyone knows that Protestants can't play football."

"Jock Stein couldn't play fitba. He was a statue. An Eastern Island statue. And he was just about as fast as an Eastern Island statue. He only ever watched training sessions. We used to do this thing. You'd run underneath the railing around the ground, with a ball at your feet, ducking and diving, under one stanchion and onto the next. Some of the big diddies like John Clark, they couldn't even get their fat bodies between one stanchion and the other. Jock. Big Jock. He'd let him sit it out. He'd let him sit it out because he was a Protestant."

"We were playing East Fife. Big fat John Clark got injured. There were no subs in those days, no trainers running on to tell the player to stay down like a dud boxer and protect their contract, or offer more money to get up and save the team. The strategy was always the same. If a player couldn't play on you moved him up front. If you couldn't kick with your left leg, you kicked with your right. And if you couldn't kick with your right leg you kicked with your left. And if you couldn't kick with either foot you got moved up front so that you could use your big ba' John Clarke heid. Even if you had to lie on the park at least you were taking up a bit of space. The one thing you never, never did, was come aff, because there was no one else to go on and you'd be letting your team mates down. Big John Clark, he took a little knock and you know what happened?"

"Yes," I said like a pantomime villain, "he went off".

"That's right," said Granda, "the fat useless bastard went aff".

"Statues don't usually talk. But I thought Big Jock might have finally had the gumption to say something. But he said nothing. I moved back to wing-back and then back further to help big Billy in defence. We were doing quite well, but then we were hit with a flurry of goals right at the end of the game. So we were fucked, but we were still top of the league.

"Big Jock didn't say anything after the game, but he was in early that Monday at Barrowfield. We had put out a few tentative feelers to see how Big Jock was feeling. A few braver ones, like big Billy, even tried addressing him directly. But it was a no-goer. Big Jock positioned himself on the training ground and was determined to show us where we had gone wrong on Saturday. Barrowfield was gravel parks. That was the Astroturf of our day. Luckily it was gravel because Big Jock didn't sink in too much. He was going to show us, but with every creek and turn he made I knocked the ball through his legs. We didn't have nutmegs in those days. But that was as close as it came. It wasn't really fair. It was like playing against traffic cones. Big Jock missed the ball every time. I tried not to laugh too much. But there was one time he didn't miss. He toed me right up the arse. That was probably his best ever volley. But I didn't feel that at the time."

"I was the aggrieved party. I was the one that had to fall back in defence because of that balloon Clark, but was I thanked for that? No I wasn't. Big Jock blamed me for the defeat."

"You were shite,' said Big Jock, breaking with Eastern Island tradition and actually talking. 'Shite. You cost us three goals."

"I didn't want to argue with him, especially since I'd never properly spoken to him before, but I was clutching my cakehole and lost it.

"'Boss, boss,' I said, 'the three goals were lost by headers. Headers!'"

"'What of it?' said a loquacious Big Jock.

"'But you call me the leprechaun boss!'

"Big Jock went back to his not talking. It would have been better if it stayed that way.

Then, just when I thought he was finished talking for that era, he said, with a face of stone: 'Aye, but leprechauns are good in the air.'

"That was my last ever game for Celtic."

After that he fell back into a deep slumber, allowing me the opportunity to sneak out.

North Sea To Seville

Chris Walter

In 2002 I was working on an oil platform in the Northern North Sea off the coast of the Shetlands with a good friend of mine and fellow Celt Mark McAdams. At the start of the football season we said we'd get to a European away game that season. We sat down and looked at the dates for the Champions League qualifier against Basel. On realising we were offshore for the away leg we hoped for a win and a chance to make the next round.

Alas, it wasn't to be, but at least this still gave us a chance of an away Euro adventure in the EUFA Cup. The next game was a trip to Lithuania but, frustratingly, we were once again denied by offshore rotas.

As if understanding our predicament the team marched through to the next round, thus giving us another bite at the European cherry.

Unfortunately, our hope of enjoying the wee trip down the road to Blackburn was stopped by our two-weeks on two-weeks off work life.

But it wasn't all doom and gloom. We watched all the games on the big TV in the helicopter departure lounge with workmates. The English fans present declared we would never get past Blackburn.

The craic was great watching the games, especially as we kept progressing.

Celta Vigo were next, but still we had to watch the away leg from the middle of the North Sea and still we progressed thanks to some great work from the boot of Henrik.

Next up we took our usual places on the couches in the Heli lounge and watched a tense away leg in Stuttgart as the team continued to march on.

Drawing Liverpool in the next round was met by "you'll not beat an English Premier side twice in the competition" from our English workmates. Again we sat in the Heli lounge offshore and watched the away leg. Like everyone who saw it, I'll never forget Hartson's goal, and thought for the first time, 'We're going all the way to the final after this result.'

Mark and I looked at the dates and saw the semi-final was a no go. The final, however, was right in the middle of our leave.

'It's fate,' I told him.

All year we had tried to get away in Europe and finally, if we got past Boavista, we were going to Seville. I went to the home leg and came away thinking it was a bit tight, but still felt confident.

As we watched the away leg from our now familiar seats in the Heli lounge on the Ninian Southern oil platform Henrik did it again. It was actually happening. We rushed to the computer and booked flights and hotels.

The day before the match we flew early morning straight into Seville. Nerves prevented us sleeping a wink the night before the flight but right after we checked in to our hotel we hit the town. In the first bar we met six lads trying to find a mechanic. They'd driven all the way from Donegal in a beat-up transit. It had died a couple of times on the journey but managed to reach Seville by sheer luck and determination, before finally retiring in the sun. None of the lads seemed too concerned on the logistics of getting home, which pretty much summed it up for a lot of fans. They just wanted to be there by any means possible. We had guys sleeping on our hotel floor and sneaked them into the restaurant for breakfast. The hotel was full of hoops and the staff couldn't tell guests from imposters.

On match day we partied in the sun with all the Bhoys and Ghirls. We met the big yin, Dermot Desmond, Billy McNeill, old mates and new mates. The main street swelled with fans to such an extent the police just shut the road. After walking around in our Celtic tartan kilts all day the heat was causing a bit of sweat rash in the nether regions. A solution was found in a local pharmacy, and the wee Spanish lassie was in fits of laughter as we liberally schooshed on the newly purchased baby powder in the shop doorway. As evening approached I started to feel sick and dizzy due to a bit of pealy-wally man's curse - sunstroke. One of the lads suggested I go back to the hotel and stand under the cold shower for as long as I could. I was a tad sceptical but it actually worked. Im still not sure if it was the cold shower, or sheer determination not to miss the game.

I won't go into the game as we all know what happened, only to say that Henrik Larsson's header to equalise is the closest I've come to messing my pants watching a football game. Even though I wasn't wearing any under my kilt, but you get the idea.

After a wee greet, some football analysis and a few beers Mark and I headed back to our hotel. Along with many Celtic fans we were quietly walking down a street when we noticed three Porto fans among us.

You could feel the tension until one Celtic fan at the back shouted to the front, "Watch they Porto fans coming up behind don't trip you, mate."

Everybody started laughing, including the three Porto fans, which pretty much summed up the feeling of the Bhoys in Seville for me.

We'd been part of a great coming together of the Celtic family and, disappointment aside, had a great time. Looking back I forget the pain of losing and prefer to remember only the good times, laughs and camaraderie of the Celtic family in those three wonderful days in Seville, and smile with pride to have played a small part in our history.

Stiliyan "Stan" Petrov

Paul Colvin

That number stood wherever he played

And in that minute, thousands prayed

No silence but applause from fans

Throughout the world for Stan The Man.

At Villa Park tears filled his eyes

The next day it was Paradise

Where sixty thousand sang his name

And banners flew throughout the game.

Respected by his peers and foes

We remembered days not long ago

This humble man, so proud, upright,

Loved to wear the green and white.

He never stopped, he'd run all day

In his peculiar, lunging way

A midfield ace with workman's flair

Who battled hard but tackled fair.

He loved a scrap, he loved a fight

Our 19 fought for all that's right

His goals would grace the greatest show

And we were sad to see him go

Though not as sad as we feel now

As Stan was dealt a hammer blow

He's battling now a force unseen

His diagnosis unforeseen.

God bless you Stan, you're in our prayers

Your family share our thoughts and cares

If God exists, let it be seen

And cure our Stan who wears 19.

Mr. Lynch

Jim Brown

As a young Bhoy, I attended St Gerard's Secondary School in Govan. First Year was another world. The school had a reputation for, well, shall we say a no-nonsense approach to discipline. Even the Orkney Street police station (right across the road) couldn't check some of the daily goings on. I had a fair idea of how things worked, though, as my older siblings attended the school.

My brother Joe told me of a Maths teacher, Mr. Lynch... Matt Lynch. He had to be at it. Matt Lynch must be ancient. But, lo and behold, there he stood teaching Maths in the annexe.

Matthew Lynch played for Celtic between '34 and '47. An honest gentleman, Matt played the game hard, but played fair. Abashed when discussing his own abilities, he was part of the legendary Exhibition Cup winning Celtic team.

Mr. O'Donnell, the P.E teacher had been on the payroll since the year zero. He kept an eye on the team with Mr. Lynch (I always addressed him as Mr, except during the game, as a mark of my genuine respect).Though small and thin, I was a goalkeeper. Because I was a gymnast, I had agility. My fiercest opposition for a spot in the school side came from Brian Nicolson, a good keeper and friend. On the Monday after my trial Mr. Lynch told me to bulk up, he had seen more meat on a butcher's pencil. He then grilled me over my homework. He gave out homework as well as he played football.

On any given day, if you fancied a break... ask about Celtic. He'd talk of the 'auld days'. Of names passed down from father to son. Names of legend: Willie Maley, Johnny Crum, Jimmy Delaney (who had replaced Mr. Lynch in the Exhibition Cup Final).

"It's about being part ae the team, lads," he said. "No about being in the team."

Malcolm MacDonald, he'd protest, was the greatest player ever seen in the hoops. Neither Dalglish, nor McGrain were better. Not even Wee Jinky

218

could measure up (although he harboured the same immense pride in the Lisbon Lions that we all do). He'd talk Tic to the extent that no work got done, hence all the homework.

The day after Celtic beat Rangers 4-2 to win the league in May '79, he didn't make it in. He loved the Old Firm, and never spoke ill of Rangers, often musing about his derby day dismissal. He received his marching orders at Ibrox in '43 in a blaze of controversy. In a fine gesture of sportsmanship, Rangers player Jimmy Duncanson had sent a handwritten note to the SFA in Matt's defence. Mr. Lynch never ran out of appraisal for his actions.

During the inter-school competition, I was keeper. Four tough wins and a draw saw us into the final. Supported by all the staff, students and parents of a large school (except for mine) four crucial saves helped me become the man of the match. One a penalty, one a back flip I never forgot. I was carried shoulder high from the park by the team and fans. I was a hero.

Later, alone in the dressing room trying to wind down, whistling flowed behind me: The Johnny Thompson Song. Mr. Lynch smiled. He gave me the well-in nod and said, "James, if only your Maths was as good as your goalkeeping!"

"I'll take that as a compliment, Mr. Lynch."

He laughed and walked away. I turned red

A friend told me Mr Lynch was the president of the Celtic Supporters Association. He served them many years, and gave good advice to those who needed it, just like in school. When he learned I was a Jungle Bhoy I got roasted.

"So it's you starting all they sing-songs when you should be studying, or goalkeeping?" He winked at me and charged on with the lesson.

Matthew Lynch died in 1999. The deaths of himself and Malky McDonald were honoured by one minute of silence. I shed a wee tear for the great man who I'd known and respected. I cheered on the Celtic in his honour. Larsson and Viduka both bagged hat-tricks in a 7-0 win.

Guys like Matt Lynch are mythical. These men played for their beloved Celtic through thick and thin, with pride and passion. They played during hard times, not for money, but for the hooped jersey, and all it represented.

"I took a trip to Parkhead...to the dear old Paradise... as the teams made..."

Well, I think I'll just whistle it one more time in memory an old friend and a great man. Rest in peace, Sir.

Jinky Magic

Lorenzo Wordsmith

Jinky weaved his magic in and out with outrageous trickery

Darting around about the tangled legs and socks of blue

They really had no clue

We rejoiced and voiced it too

The low centre of gravity from streets of tanner baw

In areas of poverty these skills and raw talents emerge

Whilst on the verge of immortality

They shine through

Directed by such men of legend

No more so than against those mortal sons in blue

Jinky weaved his way to reach the top

The world inhaled and held those breaths

Those dazzled mazy runs Un-dribbled

Journalists penned and scribbled amazement

Still this very day

Drooling over witness to this magician who shone through

He was uncanny

He specialised with ball in making example

Leaving others simply depressed and blue

No toilet breaks for any when Oor Jinky ran at you

He may be gone

He may be passed but remembered with passion new

His skills and common decency

The gentlemanly ways renew, each day for all to savour

As to his statue we all pay homage

His time here spent entertaining with his skill

His art

His love

His life was a lesson to all, who stood in stand in awe

Those that wore that ghastly shade could only appreciate that man

He chased that baw many times into and through

That hue of shallow blue

There was no defence bar capitulation

What we witnessed was folklore and oh so true

Still we compare him with the stuff of dreams

Always looking for our new Jinky it seems

Always will

For there are few that wear those colours so well

With that baw stuck on those tricky feet like glue.

Remembering the Jinky magic.

Trophy in Seville

Sean Docherty

Of course every Celtic fan has a story about Seville, we know that from our pals' stories, books released and tales on the brilliant Celtic podcasts.

My tale is a bit different. I won a trophy on the road to Seville.

I travelled to Malaga with a guy I only knew because his brother sat in front of me in Section 433. He won't thank me for reminding me he's called Basra, as he really really hates that name, but hey.

Our outward flight involved an overnight stop in Luton. Chaos ensued. We met John Hartson's best pal and a cracking lad from the Celtic Supporters Club. He led us onto several establishments, where far too many beers were downed, and treated us to a curry. Such was the festivities an early morning panicked sprint from our airport hotel to the departure gate was required. We were pretty quick for two drunken fools.

Relief. We'd made the plane to Malaga.

We were soon on the road again to our resort. We planned to stay in Benalmedena and get a bus to Seville the morning of the game. On arrival we seen hundreds of hoops already there, so we relaxed and got tore into the bevvy.

That first night in the square in Benalmedena is a bit of a blur. I woke up the next morning with no money. Thankfully, I met my savour 'Big Tony' in a nearby bar. He and his pals not only bought me, a total stranger, a load of beers, but also donated cash for a cab back to my hotel to clean up. In the face of such generosity I was so overwhelmed that, in an act of solidarity, I stole one of his gutties with a sincere promise that I'd be back with his money, post haste.

He was still in the bar hopping about on one shoe when I returned a short time later.

We shared a few beers, then mo chara Basra was on the phone wondering if I was still alive. I told him we'd meet at the watch tower. Unfortunately

223

none of us knew there were a number of these along the shore. But we got there in the end and, much to his embarrassment, I was apparently suitably fecked again. Nothing a quick dunt in the sea wouldn't fix, followed by a kickaboot with loads of hoops – well him no me. I was happy just to sit down and watch and dry out.

After that game we wandered up a wee side street and staggered into Bailleys, a small Irish bar. I nabbed a quick forty winks leaning on our fitba, which fitted neatly into the ashtray on the table.

Once rejuvenated I noticed a wee darling hustling a load of Irish guys at pool with plenty of patter. I fancied a bit of that so I put my money down and lined-up to break. Turned out to be a big break for me. We enjoyed the rest of the week together and travelled to Seville with Basra and her sister Debs.

I drank (water) and sweated like feck in the main square. We walked miles to the stadium, through the outer security cordon and through the turnstiles into the cup final - the UEFA Cup Final. We were full of excitement, anxiety and fear, but most of all pride and hope the team would do themselves justice.

They did, of course. The immense pride in our hearts was tinged with absolute disappointed...but what an experience we had shared.

We continued to enjoy a brilliant week but all good things come to an end - time to go home and back to reality. But....

Fate and Celtic fecking up the league brought us back together in Scotland, in mutual depression I admit. How can we have such a brilliant season and win nothing?

Today I'm married to Paula, the pool hustler I met on the road to Seville. We have two gorgeous kids, Megan 7 and Conor 4. Celtic continue to rule both our hearts and our kids are constantly reminded of the Celtic story and what our club means, hopefully to stand them in good stead.

So, as you can see, Celtic might have lost in Seville but there's no doubting Paula and I both won a trophy for life.

Our Special Gift

Paul Colvin

I can't explain to lesser men, they just don't comprehend

What I feel within my heart, they'll never understand

We're more than just a football club, much more than a team

With a richness money cannot buy, others only see in dreams.

Our priceless gift, received at birth and welcomed worldwide

A passport to a way of life and hallmarked Celtic Pride.

An acceptance to our family of which you are a part

You cannot buy its membership, it's built into your heart.

We sing our songs with passion 'til tears come to our eyes

But only those, who have the gift, can enter Paradise.

The Celtic Family

Tilda McCrimmon

One of the phrases which often makes me cringe is 'The Celtic Family'. It's like a nurse being described as an angel. I'm a nurse, but I'm no saint, no ethereal being. I'm a hardworking woman and the bread winner for her family.

Having said that, we are in many ways, like a family. That old saying, 'You can chose your friends but not your family' springs to mind. Similarly, you can chose to support Celtic but you can't choose your fellow supporter. At Parkhead I meet and greet, hug and sing along with people I never see at any other time. Some I look at and think they are like me and I probably have things in common with, others I look at and cannot imagine mingling with in any other situation. Love of Celtic binds us together.

The Celtic Family takes on another meaning for me. When I think of my own immediate family tales of Celtic run through our history. My mum, unusual for her generation, was a great football fan. She always maintained, though, that my Dad only took her along so she could roll his fags while he drove to the match. My Dad told how, after the win in Lisbon, my Gran said to him and my uncle if she had known they wanted to go she would have helped pay. She then helped to pay for the trip to Milan. My brothers tell of being lifted over turnstiles and hoisted on to my Dad's shoulders to watch the match.

As a parent raising a family in the West of Scotland I consciously did not instil Celtic into my sons. Like religion I felt they should chose for themselves. Alas, one trip to Paradise with his Gran and my son was hooked and soon had his own season ticket.

Winning the Celtic pools, which their uncle bought for them, was one of the great memories of his and his cousins' childhood. £500 was a lot of money for a 10 year old. He was also always lucky with ticket ballots and his name came out of the hat more times than not. Getting a ticket for Seville from the ballot was his luckiest day.

So at eighteen off he went on the 72 hour bus trip. As his mammy I made sure he had sun cream, toothpaste, map of Seville and anything else my maternal instincts could think of. He returned from Seville with horrendously cracked lips, which made me feel really guilty about not sending him off with some lip salve. He confessed six months later that, rather than the scorching Spanish sun, he had failed to blow out a Sambuca properly and burnt his lips.

My husband and I have a tradition of both forgetting our wedding anniversary, usually remembering about a week later. So I surprised myself by seeing my off-duty at work and I requested the day off to celebrate our 10th wedding anniversary. No, wait a minute, that's not quite true. I requested 21/11 for the home game against Manchester United. Needless to say we celebrated our anniversary on the 22nd.

My mum's life was cut short by cancer, yet even while she was dying Celtic featured in our lives. The home tie against Barcelona, the night we heard her diagnosis, was surreal. How could we watch this match with such awful news hanging over us. But the rendition, one of the most beautiful ever, of You Will Never Walk Alone dedicated to the victims of the Madrid bombings gave me strength. By the away leg, she was getting frailer and I feel privileged that I sat and watched the game with her and her sisters.

The defeat in Villareal seemed to mark a rapid deterioration in her condition. I am sure an oncologist would tell me that there was a physiological reason for this, but I will always feel, with the European adventure over, she felt she didn't need to struggle on.

My sister-in-law wrote to Celtic to tell them that one of their lifelong fans was dying. Corporate sent a pre-printed, get-well card. Steam coming from her ears my sister-in-law got on the phone. This family had paid Celtic thousands through the years, good and bad, and a lousy pre-printed card was all the club could offer. Two days later my Mum received a signed card from our beloved Henrik Larsson, which certainly made her day and sat proudly at the centre of all her cards. As a special dispensation her parish priest allowed her coffin to leave the church with You Will Never Walk Alone. A request normally turned down, but granted in recognition that she had been a devout Catholic as well as a devout Celtic supporter.

Having put this all down I will never cringe again. Not only am I part of The Celtic Family I come from a Celtic Family.

Farewell Joe McBride

J J Whelan

Sad news came over at 10 O'clock

I thought this can't be true

A Celtic legend's gone to sleep

And joined the immortal crew

He's gone to join those famous men

Johnstone, Murdoch and Mr. Stein

To reminisce with that special squad

Whose likes shall never be seen

Prolific goalscorer of his game

Part of that famous '67 team

Although he never played that day

Lisbon's where he lived the dream

Joe McBride has passed away

A man of quality and style

This genius and true professional

Played with eloquence and guile

The Celtic family is now in mourning

As they say goodbye to a famous son

In our prayers and in our thoughts

We bid farewell to a special one....

Promise Me

TBK

Like many others of the era my wee Granny was a devout Catholic, attending mass every day she was physically able, or, invariably, mass came to her home. Despite the harshness of life she was never a bitter woman, remaining kind, generous and forgiving, with a disarming smile. But behind that smile lay a truth unafraid to reveal itself.

On nights holding court, as she often did of a family event, particularly Christmas or New Year, she'd tell those gathered how the family travelled to Scotland in the cattle boat, with no money to speak of and only the clothes on their backs as a claim to property.

First-footing neighbours, aunts, uncles, all branches of family tree, would gather round sharing the whiskey, the lump of coal and a well-versed story or song often ending in warming tears. These songs and stories were told in the 'traditional' manner. As folk crammed into the living room in front of an open fire she'd sit with a 'Jamieson' in hand.

Originally from the North of Ireland, her family, like many, many other families, were burnt out of their home by the Black and Tans for no other reason than strong faith or political beliefs. I used to listen, transfixed on every word, every proud emotion. These were my tales of inheritance.

But it wasn't all doom and gloom of oppression. She often regaled us with tales of a movement that filled her and countless others with hope and pride. A movement formed to help her family, and others like hers, be part of something bigger than them, yet part of them. That movement was Celtic Football Club.

Celtic stood alone as champions of the poor Irish immigrants in Glasgow's East End. At a time when many native Scots were hostile to newcomers Celtic showed the way. They were as good, if not better, than anyone when it came to understanding all the needs of the Scottish and Irish Catholic working classes. And it was Celtic, through playing football, who put smiles on thousands of men, women and children every week.

My Granny summed-up the relationship between the club and the people. 'We are all one family. Our suffering is their suffering , their strength is our strength.'

In her early years Granny cleaned houses for the local wealthy folk. I don't recall her ever having a proper job. Old-fashioned as it now seems, Granddad's role was to work and provide for his family, but he also drove my Granny to her job for pin money.

Granny was sixteen and Granddad seventeen when they first met. She was Roman Catholic of strong Irish stock; he was from Ayrshire of Orange/Protestant stock. He was a man of the "rifles", a third Lanark man. Both families 'strongly' disapproved of their connection, but they didn't care. They were, after all, in love, and love would see them through. They followed their hearts, eloped, soon married and started a family.

Granddad's family, in protest, disowned him. Granddad, to his credit, stood firm in his love of wife and loss of family, but no doubt, with silent personal regret. He stayed true to himself and, of course, my Granny. I have a deep sense of pride for him, for that couldn't have been easy.

She never travelled anywhere unless Granddad drove her, because that's how it was meant to be. They were as close as pickles in a jar. He would chauffer her to mass every day and sit outside that holy house in the car waiting. Sometimes, as we lived close-by, he came to our house for a cup of tea and smoke. He'd discuss football and Celtic results with my Da. I noticed they didn't get on too well, but still they tried; cast from the same mould they say. When it was near the time for mass coming out he'd bid us goodbye and fetch is beloved.

Occasionally my Granny would walk back to the house from Mass, if it had perhaps finished early, or maybe there was a visiting priest, or, sometimes, to catch highlights of Celtic on television.

In those days there wasn't much live football on TV. The occasional cup final or, latterly, highlights on a Sunday evening. It was then I witnessed my Granny in 'Celtic' mode.

I'd sit and laugh as she'd sit and shout. "C'mon the Bhoys."

We'd all respond in kind to this elderly 'capo' leading the chants. Such nights helped me understand the importance of Celtic. The church may have helped fill our souls with grace but Celtic filled our hearts with hope and joy.

My Granny and Granddad shared their lives together, inseparable for over 60 years, until that quiet man, her partner, her love, her most trusted driver, my Granddad, received his last rites. This man, who'd lived his life without religion, having witnessed the devotion and comfort it brought to his lifelong partner, converted to her religion on his dying bed.

I thought broken hearts a convenient excuse to become reclusive, or sulk, or retreat within oneself. I believe differently now. The loving heart can indeed be broken; broken to the point where life itself is not a life but a waiting for death.

My wee Granny never recovered from her loss and died less than a year later. Her last words to me were, "Listen, son. I don't really mind if you never go to church again, that is your decision, but promise me, promise me, you will always be Celtic."

And, of course, I do remain to this day true to that promise. For to be anything other would be sacrilegious.

Lennon The Man

J J Whelan

Destined to be one of us, fine sportsman in his day

Now he's here to lead us, in each and every way

A man who stands by morals, the hoops he wore with pride

Such passion for this great club, for which he cannot hide

Taken knocks along the way, his share of mortal strife

Bombs and bullets did not deter, for Celtic's now his life

Media have tortured him, in times of discontent

Does he turn the other cheek, or treat them with contempt

The Man they call Lennon, will reside here for a while

"His day has come", now to laugh, and beam a victorious smile.

Soldiers Are We

Connor McCallum

This Coontin' Hoose is fuckin rockin, man. Bet it's no like this every Saturday morning. Ah'm quite rockin masel. They spliffs are fair tangling wae this early bevy. That clock up there's awready looking hazy. Ah make it...Ah make it...quarter past twelve. Ah need tae lean on the wet bar top tae centre masel. A bit ae anchorage helps. 'Cheers hen,' Ah say tae the lassie hawnin me ma change. She's awright lookin, in that 'no wan fur takin hame tae meet yir maw' sorta wey. Ah pick up the four pints 'n' turn tae a roarin sea ae ma comrades aw dressed in green and white finery.

Thir's a couple ae right auld geezers in the corner givin it a bit ae the chantin. Ah'm no the strongest wae the tunes anywey, never mind the background noise, but Ah cin make oot *'from the land beyond the sea'*.

A group ae breakfast-eaters uhr shakin thir heids 'n' shruggin at each other, clueless tae the point n purpose behind this grand clan gatherin. That's aw we want the day - numbers. Lots ae them. Mind you, by the look ae this place that willnae be a problem. It's like the fuckin London underground in here.

It's a bit ae a struggle but Ah finally get back tae oor spot n dish oot the pints tae the day's adopted uncles. Ah need tae hawd on tae the auld yin's, though, coz he's on wan ae eez walkaboots, man. Nae doubt he'll be chinnin away tae any n everybody.

"Wit time's this kickin' aff at again?" Tony asks, staggerin intae Callum who, in turn, bums intae the group ae lads beside him.

Wan ae the group turns roon wae a Begbie look on his face, but it's awright. He's no lookin' fur any trouble. He throws an arm roon Callum and starts singing, *"Oh, I am a merry ploughboy..."*

We're laughin along 'til the auld man squeezes in tae oor patch, lifts his pint 'n' gies me a pat on the back. "This is what it's aw aboot, son."

"Whit? Pints ae Carling?"

He knows Ah'm just being wide coz Ah can feel wan ae eez spiels comin' on. He's bad enough sober but efter a couple a jars he's a nightmare.

"These lads in here. Look at the different generations. Different backgrounds. Aw wae wan thing in common..."

Ah try tae head him aff at the pass. "Aye, thir aw swatchin' that wee darlin behind the bar."

The old man laughs. "Aye, fair enough.... two hings in common. They aw understawn Celtic are mer than a football club. They understawn who we are 'n' where we come fae. The struggles o'er the years for an equal wage. Discrimination instead ae opportunity. That's why they're here the day, son. Maist here probly know mer people in the fire brigade than in the Green Brigade. But that disnae matter. Whit they see is Celtic supporters... wae that shared heritage... dealin wae the sorta harassment thir ain fathers wir put through. The sort that shouldnae exist in a so-called modern, multicultural state."

Ah nod and raise ma gless, hawf ae me appreciating his point, hawf ae me gled he'd made it in less than three oors.

Ah wis in two minds aboot whether or no tae come tae this the day. Ah'm Celtic by blood, man, but Ah've never been intae the republican hing or anyhin like that. The socialist in me says it's corrosive tae the workin class whole, ye know? No on its ain mind you. Unionism is just the same. And Ah suppose if yir gonnae cram opposing ideologies intae the wan city wae two fitba teams as poster boys, yir gonnae huv trouble. No that Ah'm tryin tae justify trouble. Ah think cunts fae any side should be alood tae dae thir fuckin thing, man. It's a freedom a speech issue. Let the people sing 'n' aw that. That goes fur baith sides.

At first Ah'd thought that the whole persecution vibe goin aboot wis just the usual Celtic paranoia. Ah thought it wis aw aboot a bunch a daft wee neds gettin' caught and then greetin' aboot it. And tae be honest, Ah couldnae really give a fuck.

Then Ah fun oot Danny's story. He hud nae criminal record, yet in November 2010 he wis arrested fir 'Sectarian Breach ae the Peace'.

Sixteen months ae judicial fuckaboutery led tae a no guilty verdict. The time aff he'd been forced tae take meant the cunt lost his fuckin job. His fuckin job, man. His offense had been huvin his hawn on a banner showing Lennon in front ae a burnin' Ibrox. The Celtic manager, in front ae the Rangers hame ground in flames just isnae a sectarian image, it's fitba banter. The pope in front ae a burnin' Westminster Abbey, wid be sectarian.

Ah then phoned ma Da and he told me aboot Dion. Dion wis arrested 'n' held o'ernight in Dundee, under Mr. Salmond's new flagship bill: The Offensive Behaviour at Football and Threatening Communications Act. Basically, the guy, who hud never been in trouble at the fitba, got charged wae singin a rebel tune. His name got splashed aw o'er the tabloids, who distortit the facts 'n' made him oot a hooligan. A lifelong fan, he wis noo banned fae aw Celtic games. He went tae court 'n' wis found no guilty, aboot which the press wir very fuckin' quiet indeed.

Efter that Ah fun oot aboot a few mer cases and couldnae believe whit Ah heard aboot Chris.

Chris, a public servant, again wae nae criminal record, wis arrested comin' hame fae holiday wae his burd. Four ae Glesga's finest cuffed 'n' dragged him ootae a line of returning travellers at Glasgow Airport. His poor missus wis in some nick watchin it, anaw. When he asked the polis why they'd got him at the airport they said is wis because he'd moved 'n' they didnae know where he lived noo.

"Fair enough, officer," he said. "But you know where I sit at matches, where I drink beforehand 'n' no doubt how I get to games. So, again, why the airport?"

Nane ae them responded tae this question, but the answer's clear. Tae humiliate the cunt. He wis charged wae huvin his hawn on a banner but the case wis thrown oot afore it reached court. It turned oot they'd nae evidence. Nae evidence ataw.

Ah wis uplifted tae hear that a small group ae fans hud got thegither, organised a cheeky protest march, banners 'n' all, fae thir usual waterin hole tae Paradise. Aboot seventy marched that day fir thir right tae freedom ae expression, freedom ae protest. Tae highlight persecution they marched. Tae cheer the team thit wis founded, aw they years ago, against discrimination. Ah had nae intention ae joining them or anyhin but wis proud that they wur dain somethin.

Then the news started tricklin' oot that day.

They'd turned a corner doon the Gallowgate 'n' were kettled in by three hunner polis and a mounted division. Photies showed a bunch ae fifteen year aulds 'n' in wan case a wee lassie under ten gettin some right fuckin hassle. No wan photy ae the polis pickin on adult men.

Well that wis fuckin it fir me. Nae group should be treated how they bhoys wir treated. Every Celtic fan couldnae possibly share aw the same beliefs, the net's been cast far too wide fir 'at but, fuck... Wit's the words again? Ah might no agree wae everyhin' ye say, but Ah'll die defendin yir right tae say it? Wan phone call tae the auld man confirmed ah wis ready tae stawn up 'n' be counted.

We head ootside tae George Square just as the FAC guy gets up on the pedestal tae start speakin so, leavin the auld yins in ma wake, Ah jump up a statue for a proper swatch ae the mob.

The sun's illuminatin a green 'n' white ocean. Banners ae all sorts bobble aboot like buoys on the water. Going by the banners thir's a good turnoot ae supporters groups. 'Fans Against Criminalisation' picket signs uhr everywhere anaw 'n' some that say 'End Fan Harassment' against a backdrop ae they disgustin kettlin photos. Thir's a fuckin quality vibe in the air.

We aw go silent as the guy starts layin it doon.

'THIS LEGISLATION...is not only UNJUST...it's UNNECESSARY! And it's PLAIN WRONG!'

Every cunt cheers 'n' it's a proper wall of sound, man. He keeps drivin it home aboot the Act, 'n' the crowd keep roarin at aw the right bits. They don't look yir typical protest crowd but thir spirited and wid put any self-proclaimed activist tae shame. Ah cannae mind the Square ever bein this busy. Thir's easily mair than three thousand here. Another couple ae speakers come on 'n' dae thir bits well. Ah jist stawn up on the statue watchin the crowd, lovin the left-wing rhetoric 'n' fir the first time, graspin wit Ah wis always telt it wis aw aboot. A club formed tae represent the impoverished 'n' oppressed people. Ma people.

Next up on the platform, Jeanette Findlay fae the Celtic Trust sends oot a message tae the polis: 'If you try to beat us off the streets, we will keep coming back in bigger and bigger numbers, until you have not enough truncheons and horses and dogs to keep us down, and you don't have enough bodies to kettle and constrain us.'

The rally finishes 'n' we're a river, flowin through the city like a flash flood. A mix ae Celtic songs 'n' political chants wash through the city centre en route. Behind me, aw Ah see is Celtic tops, and the same in front.

'HERE WE GO AGAIN! WE'RE ON THE ROAD AGAIN!'

We come tae the spot where it aw went doon wae the seventy bold yins afore. Well, fuckin kettle us noo, ya dicks! But thir's nae real polis presence th-day even though this impromptu march husnae been officially sanctioned. The cunts've shat it, which is probably just as well. Ah'm here tae make a point, no tae get lifted.

'WHAT THE HELL DO WE CARE!? WHAT THE HELL DO WE CARE!?'

It's only quarter past two so Ah grab the auld man 'n' we slink intae the Sarry Heid. As he dishes oot the pints he jabs ma arm 'n' points at me, in that aboot tae impart wisdom wey, 'n' says, "It'll be remembered, son, that when the call tae fight against injustice came on the 6th April 2013...the Celtic wur there. The club steeped in..."

"Ah get it, Da. Ah Get it. And Ah can feel it tae. Believe me, Ah can feel it. Yir right, it's in the blood 'n' aw that. Noo get that pint doon ye."

In the corner thir's three auld codgers givin it laldy, "North men, South men, comrades all..."

A Day with the Green Brigade

Joe McKenna

There are any number of ways I could start this but I think it's best to quote one of the many Green Brigade members I met in Section 111.

"As I was walking here I spotted a copper that we're all familiar with and he asked me, 'How did your demonstration go?' I says, 'Went great, no trouble at all. Not one bit.' He just nodded his head, so I says to him, 'Why do you think that was?' He says, 'What do you mean?' I says, 'Why do you think there was no trouble this time?' He replied, 'I don't know, I wasn't there.' I just looked at him and said, 'Exactly.'"

Many layers of mystique have been applied to the Green Brigade by writers with zero knowledge or experience of the group. A lot would have you believe the GB are a secret society, hell bent on being outsiders with a chip on their shoulder. Others want you to imagine them as marauding thugs whose sole purpose is to cause upset and discourse wherever they go.

Arriving in Glasgow Central I made my way to the Fans Against Criminalisation demo at George Square unsure what awaited me. I had been granted a privilege - a day with the Green Brigade. Would I be faced with scepticism for being, essentially, a tourist in their midst? Would I have a struggle on my hands trying to engage them in conversation? The answers weren't long in coming.

Arriving at the demo I was introduced to a senior member who couldn't have been more welcoming. I then chatted to another member for around twenty minutes, hearing stories of police intimidation, harassment, members who'd been arrested upon returning from holiday and front doors being kicked in. What struck me most was that this particular member, this very articulate, friendly and intelligent guy who was to accompany me from George Square towards Celtic Park for the game against Hibs, couldn't actually go beyond the bottom of the Gallowgate due to a banning order. To me he came across as a guy who would have to try very hard to get banned from a library let alone a football stadium.

As we reached his 'no go' zone I was introduced to another member who would walk me all the way to Celtic Park, stopping only for a quick pint for me and a coke for him. We talked about the incredible scrutiny the Green Brigade have endured and the underhanded tactics used to provoke and disrupt them. We constantly shook our heads in silence in a 'What's all this about?' sort of way.

We reached Celtic Park around twenty minutes before kick-off and I took my place behind the now famous Green Brigade banner that sits proudly in Section 111. I was introduced to several members standing near me and, in all honesty, I've never been so warmly received inside Celtic Park in my life. In fact, I've never been so warmly received at a football match in my life. I shook hands with lots of people and the immediate sense of camaraderie within the section was incredible. Almost everyone who passed me on their way up the steps was greeted with pats on the back, handshakes and full bear hugs. Lads as young as ten, and maybe younger, all engaging in the most jovial manner as they prepared to do what they do best: bring an atmosphere to a stadium that is known for its character. Looking behind me I could see people of all ages, colours, creeds and sexes embracing one another. Calling it a party atmosphere would be a disservice. At most parties you'll find pockets of people doing their own thing, but this, this was a family get together. This was something that quite clearly meant an awful lot to the people around me. Not a cross word spoken and nothing but smiles all round. I couldn't have been happier. I never got the chance to experience the Jungle in my youth, but this was the next best thing and I was determined to enjoy every last second no matter what it took out of me.

I'd like to intersperse my story with tales of what was happening on the pitch but, to be honest, I can remember very little of the action. My heart was in the party and within minutes of the kick-off my feet left the ground as Section 111 burst into life. Resistance was futile. I can't imagine anyone not wanting to join in.

I looked around to the sections nearest 111 and saw many young men, eyes fixed on the Green Brigade, and I knew full well that all they wanted was for others around them to stand up and join in. Fans craned necks to get a glimpse of the smiling hive of green and white that is the Green Brigade. I saw a lad dancing alone, oblivious to the people sitting on their hands all around him. He didn't care, it's what he came to do. Perhaps, with a few more like-minded individuals, he might be able to set up another sub-section and they can have themselves the same rooting tooting time like us in 111. The Green Brigade carried the party atmosphere through to half time. Any lull in proceedings was met with an instant demand for more. Two members with megaphones were determined to keep the pot boiling at all costs.

I'd be lying if I didn't admit that come half time I was ready for a kip. I haven't jumped around like that since I hired a bouncy castle for my daughter's birthday party, drank too much and couldn't physically get myself off it. But my adrenaline was high and my cheek bones were sore from smiling. Such was the fun in the second half I almost got cramp in my face.

Anyone there will tell you the sight of the Craig Whyte banner was the highlight of the game. As it was passed around the stadium, including just under the directors box, the entire stadium shouted 'Up, up, up.' I don't think anyone really expected it to cross the sacred sofa chairs in the Main Stand, but some fans were determined to see it do just that. And when it did cross the sea of suits and ties, the cry was, 'Gie it to the Lawwell, gie it to the Lawwell' and the applause was one of warmth as the PLC swallowed their pride and joined the fans in having a good time. A good time that started in Section 111 no less.

When injury time came around my palms were sore from clapping, my legs were sore from jumping and I sounded like Frank Butcher from pushing my singing voice to its limit when belting out Roll of Honour, the Celtic Song, Discoland and the fantastically received Craig Whyte's Fenian Army. Among all this I'd forgotten about news filtering through of the Motherwell v St Mirren score. The league celebrations would have to wait, but the regular, passionate celebrations within Section 111 could not be quelled with such news. The Green Brigade did what they came to do. They had done what they always come to do and they did it with everything they had. I descended the steps of 111 inspired. I'd just spent time with a group of Celtic supporters who had given me the experience

I'd always wanted at Celtic Park. I'd always wanted to jump around, sing, dance and embrace fellow Tims and that's what I got.

I firmly expected to fill this article with stories of over-policing and tense stand-offs, but none of that happened. There were no crowds of high vis jackets bearing down on Section 111 in a bid to keep order and protect. Some speculated that perhaps things were set to change now the voices of the oppressed were being heard publicly. But what was more important, or what struck me as more important, was that with the reduced policing at this game and the Green Brigade in full voice there was not one incident of trouble. Not one tear shed, not one moment of anarchy. Nothing but explosive green and white passion. These fans, like us all, police themselves. During the moshing (that dreaded activity we've been told is so dangerous) I saw several people crowd surf, fall over and wind up far from their seats and upside down, but I also saw at least five people reaching out helping hands, and all this with riotous laughter emanating from all around. What I saw was a community of people with a combined ideal; to bring life to the football.

If you'd have seen the whole stadium doing the huddle, the Craig Whyte banner traveling the stadium and the way in which the Green Brigade will ceaselessly roar in unison in an attempt to spread passion through the support on match day then you will have been in no doubt that the fans in Section 111 are a necessity. And if you're a FoCus group member or a member of Strathclyde Police I can only defer you to a great Belfast man who sang about how his momma told him 'Everyday is like this'.

Celtic: A Work Of Art

Lorenzo Wordsmith

Celtic supporters are undoubtedly the most creative, colourful, determined, vocal, entertaining and expressive body of supporters anywhere on God's planet.

It's in the genes; my mother told me so, and I believed her. The fusion of Irish and Scottish talent combines to create a people rich in music, art and drama. Oh, and the patter's not too bad either; the recent 'Fannygate' fiasco being a point in case.

Celtic writing can be political, satirical, historical, relevant, informative, challenging, factual, poetic, strong and passionate. It can be transmitted by a simple few lines of love to express where and why it first became apparent, and what it means to you.

In banner message, picture form or musical video it is second to none when conveying the message of hope or, at times, distress. These avenues of expression remind us of the challenges our forefathers faced. They serve to educate upcoming generations so they may, armed with stories of inequality or hope, seek equal standard as their right.

The Celtic voice is far reaching and potent. It is a voice only a fool chooses to ignore or mock, yet here in Scotland there seems no shortage of such fools, but still we live in hope.

These creative styles will not be oppressed such is their potency, and these skills are produced in all manner of format. Skills which are the well-honed tools on which debate is created and solution may be found on all range of subjects pertinent to one's own Celtic perception, or indeed the universal.

They can be hard hitting and relentless, but also embracing and charitable, depending on how the times treat them, as has historically been seen, cast as a lower-level citizen, dare I say nuisance.

These artistic creations bring hope and, yes, at times, chastisement.

They empower us, though, with renewed strength and remind of a future we demand based on equality, community and recognition. We do so remembering our charitable root; a root that will forever be the top priority.

Those who project the Celtic-minded as a scourge or an underclass, or who reject us as unworthy or unimportant, would, but for our voices and words defying that assertion in such artistic ways produced with quality in communication, so skilled and natural, undoubtedly have their way.

The age old media ways that managed to hold sway, particularly on how the wider public view the society in which we live or suffer are at a loss as to how to control such a challenging voice, unaware that that voice, through many avenues as relayed, cannot, will not, be silenced.

The one thing the Celtic heart does better than any other is expression. We state our feelings and emotions, challenge what we see as wrong, unify and stand together.

The difference of the 'Rebel' from the 'Follow', you see.

An example of the follower is being played out for all to see with no sign of rebellion to lead a way from the deepening mire worsening by the day due to the blind instinct to simply follow.

We Celts rebel until the correct road to follow is found, and we do so by our expressive artistry, we communicate until the best way forward is agreed. We allow all opinion, our diversity is our strength.

These days of new media or social media, have been grabbed by the undercarriage and hoisted to a plateau that in time will be insurmountable for those that wish to protect inequality whilst proclaiming the fairest society.

You see, poor Timmy is actually rich in moral fibre. He was born with it.

Those old ways, old days are gone, the days of superior gait, of they know best, they that cling onto that past, just don't know it yet.

Celtic supporters, with good cause, see themselves and their root as victims, whether it be in work or in play. They no longer accept paranoia as an acceptable explanation, so they sing it, write it and display it, they refuse to give in, give up, or accept they are unworthy of the same rights offered to anyone else. They 'Celtic supporters' hold their history precious, offering it a place in the future, and rebel at the thought of that right being denied.

Do we feel victimisation based on religion or race? Well it could and is argued so, it has done for so very long. There does seem to be a significantly harsh difference in the treatment of those like myself who over many years have felt those differences. We all have our own personal or collective experiences.

So yes, Paddy was my Grandfather's name, and yes I am a Fenian.

I have often been reminded so from those that care to be bothered by it and not too often in the flattering term, although when asked or described so, I have never felt the urge to deny such, for with that welcome burden I am also proud. I know of none that are not.

One has to wonder if any authority that might have this fine Celtic strength silenced wherever it may be thought menacing, on this suffocating and dysfunctional planet, could have selected a more creative or strong force to challenge with a view to silencing it for the so-called greater good.

The Celtic people have always prevailed through their arts. Their messages in word and music have grown throughout history, never stronger than right now, through new media.

History may point to a titanic and catastrophic blunder and a turning point for those of old ideals, mostly due to this new media. This is why there appears to be strong movement, especially in the football sense, to close down certain freedoms.

Expression, speech and movement in the year 2013, all seem to be taking a hit with newly-created laws that threaten each of them, strangely enough on the cusp of so-called Independence. These expressions are the basic functions of freedom and so, of true Independence, but what do I know?

If one cannot really stop those freedoms the alternative I suppose would then be to silence them, at least to a degree, it's an age-old method I guess. Don't let them get too big for their boots.

The Celtic voice, though, is very strong.

The years of degradation and vilification have bolstered resentment and, in so doing, strengthened deep resolve. The artistry has grown into an expressive, enriched and potent outlet, one which pours forth emotion and unity, one which assists its charitable beginning, and continues in that vein.

Speech and expression.

With the rise of new media I'm convinced those freedoms cannot ever be denied. For using the skills, art and abilities we are blessed with, in music, in song, in dance, in sign and scribe, the voices continue to ring loud and clear. Haven't they always, won't they always?

We are Celtic you see, we are proud and we will forever be heard. Celtic is a family, a living breathing entity, and a most masterful work of art.

Walfrid's Boon

John C Traynor

Born of squalor ... mouths to feed;

born to meet a mighty need;

Sligo scholar sowed the seed

- reaped a harvest,

launched a creed.

Symbol of Hibernia's cause:

migrant generation lost.

Alba's bounty, Erin's cost

- Harp and Thistle,

karmas crossed.

Ravaged by An Gorta Mór,

blighted still on Scotia's shore;

abject underclass deplored

- godforsaken

enclave horde.

Branded, ridiculed and scorned;

shorn of dignity ... forlorn;

bigotry their crown of thorns

- race discrimination

borne.

Brute affliction spawned a club;

fulcrum of their life ... its hub;

of their soul the very nub

–roused their spirit,

raised them up.

Blessed in legend, steeped in lore;

all-inclusive open door;

oozing craic from every pore

- charity

the very core.

Quinn, McGrory, Larsson, Stein,

Maley, Lennon wove the dream:

icons of our 'Grand Old Team'

- few of many,

ever green.

Sprawling saga, epic-strewn;

heart from generations hewn;

eulogised in verse and tune

- Hail 'The Celtic',

Walfrid's Boon!

Celtic Anthology

Acknowledgements

Lorenzo Wordsmith, Jim McGinley and Pat Marrinan provided the creativity that sparked the idea for an anthology of stories and poems relating to Celtic Football Club.

Wullie Broon from TCN Web Development designed and implemented the Celtic Anthology website and social media marketing strategy. http://thecelticnetwork.co.uk/#

Jack O'Donnell provided an expert eye and hours of his time during the editing process.

Connor McCallum and Ryan Cassidy assisted with the editing.

Barry McGonigle designed the front and back covers.

David Harper helped format the book for publication.

Jim McGinley guided us through the legal minefield of setting up a company.

Many fans submitted pieces for the project. There was too many to include them all in the book.

Everyone who wished the project success, shared links to promote it or bought the book.

Finally, a huge personal thanks to Yvonne for always being supportive throughout the many months spent putting this project together.

Printed in Great Britain
by Amazon.co.uk, Ltd.,
Marston Gate.